A Level Playing Field

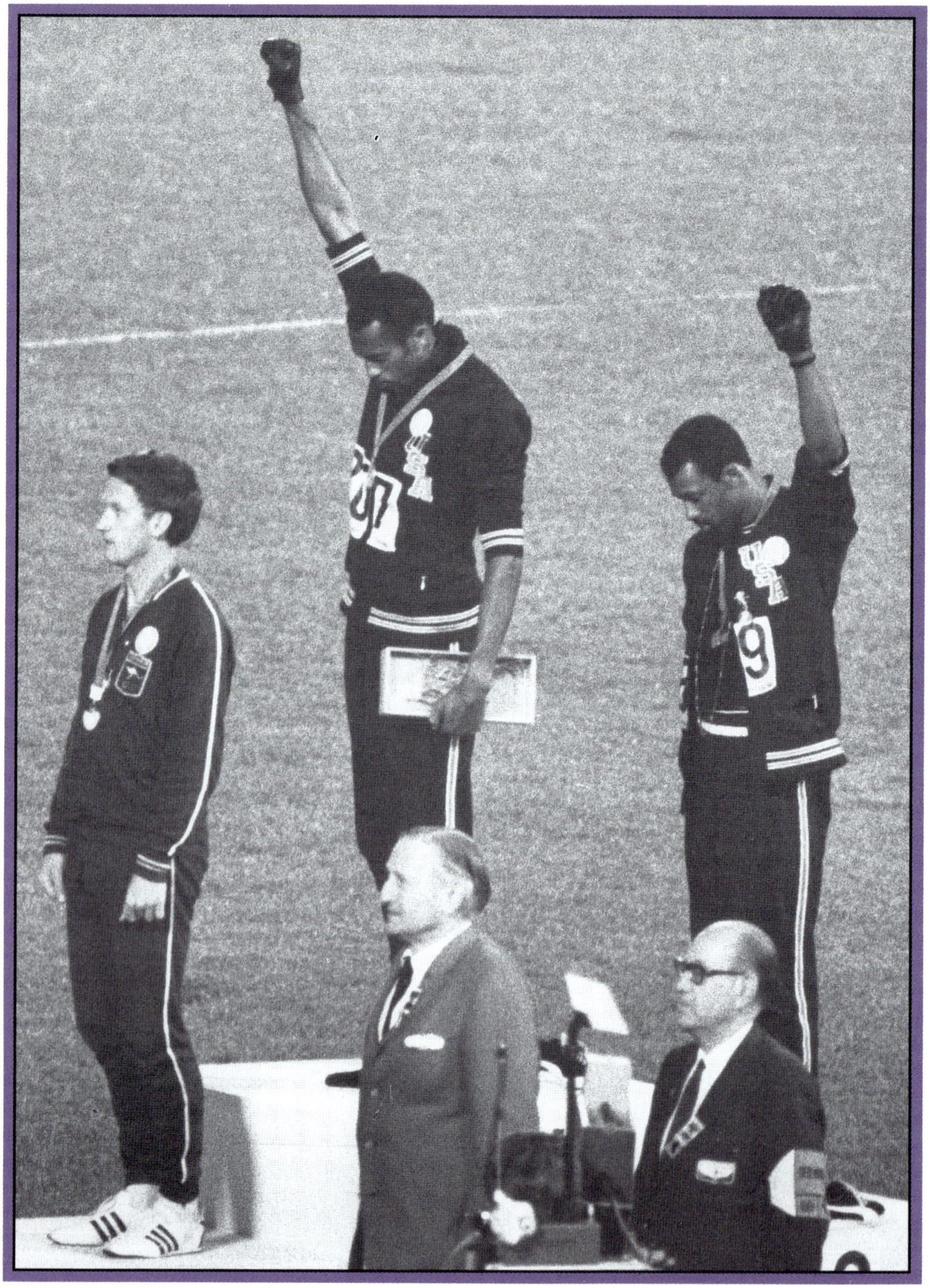

A Level Playing Field

SPORTS and RACE

EVALEEN HU

Lerner Publications Company ■ Minneapolis

*This book is dedicated
to my family*

Page 2: Medalists Tommie Smith (center) and John Carlos (right) make a stand for civil rights at the 1968 Olympics.

Copyright © 1995 by Lerner Publications Company

All rights reserved. International copyright secured. No part of this book may be reproduced or transmitted in any form or by any means, electronic or mechanical, including photocopying and recording, or by any information storage or retrieval system, without permission in writing from Lerner Publications Company, except for the inclusion of brief quotations in an acknowledged review.

Library of Congress Cataloging-in-Publication Data

Hu, Evaleen.
    A level playing field : sports and race / Evaleen Hu.
      p. cm.
    Includes bibliographical references and index.
    ISBN 0–8225–3302–2
    1. Discrimination in sports—United States—Juvenile literature.
2. Afro-American athletes—Juvenile literature. [1. Discrimination in sports—History. 2. Afro-Americans—Sports—History.]
    I. Title.
GV706.32.H8 1995
796'.089'96073—dc20   94–31516

Manufactured in the United States of America

1 2 3 4 5 6 – I/JR – 00 99 98 97 96 95

CONTENTS

1   Breaking the Color Barrier 6
2   Typecasting. 28
3   Who's in Charge? 37
4   Beyond the Playing Field. 48
5   Broken Promises 64
6   The Price of Admission. 77
     Notes *88*
     Bibliography *90*
     Index *93*

CHAPTER ONE

BREAKING THE COLOR BARRIER

When African-American sprinter James Cleveland "Jesse" Owens crossed the finish line in the 100-meter race at the 1936 Olympic Games in Berlin, Germany, he did more than prove he was the fastest man in the world. He shattered a racial barrier.

Before the games, German Nazi leader Adolf Hitler had said that white, northern European athletes would win the most medals, showing the world that whites were the superior race. Owens proved that theory wrong over and over. He won gold medals in the 100- and 200-meter races, the 400-meter relay, and the long jump. He was the only one out of 893 track and field athletes at the Games to win more than one gold medal.

Owens had faced prejudice and segregation before he went to the Olympics. In his childhood home of Alabama and in other southern states, African Americans were required to use separate movie theaters and bathrooms, attend different schools, and live in different neighborhoods than whites. Sports teams were segregated throughout the country. By earning gold medals at the Games,

SPORTS AND RACE 7

Jesse Owens took one gold medal after another at the 1936 Games.

Owens showed Hitler, the United States, and the rest of the world that black people had abilities equal to whites.

When Owens returned to the United States, he was hailed as an Olympic hero. Although professional sports remained segregated, the victories of Owens and other black athletes at the Berlin Games inspired young African Americans to become athletes. They developed a presence on college campuses, seeing track as a ticket to stardom and a good education.

The history of 20th century sports is filled with stories of groundbreaking athletes such as Owens who set records and broke color barriers. They are stories of courage and perseverance, of athletes who took risks and achieved not only for themselves but also for the cause of civil rights.

What happens on the playing field often reflects society. When Jesse Owens won four gold medals, the United States was heavily segregated, and African Americans were considered second-class citizens at best. As the racial climate improved in the United States, so did opportunities for minorities in sports.

Not only a mirror of American society, sports also has helped awaken society to racial problems. Athletes have taken stands on and off the playing field, using their fame to draw attention to racial injustice.

Because of courageous athletes and the civil rights movement of the 1950s and 1960s, the sports world has changed dramatically since Owens's victories. The complexion of basketball, baseball, and football teams has changed. Minorities have also made their mark in golf, tennis, boxing, and track and field. In the 1990s, minority athletes have more opportunities than ever. Still, the playing field is not yet level. Though minority athletes have won many battles, the struggle for racial equality continues.

A NEW BALL GAME

Well into the 20th century, American sports teams were segregated. Black basketball players staffed all-black teams like the Harlem Globetrotters. Black baseball players were confined to the Negro leagues. They showed the white sports world that minority athletes had at least as much to offer as white athletes. But professional sports teams resisted integration, fearing that white fans wouldn't pay to see athletes of any other race play.

There were a few exceptions. Some light-skinned Hispanics were accepted in major-league baseball. Jim Thorpe, a member of the Sauk and Fox Indian tribes, played professional baseball and football after earning gold medals in track and field at the 1912 Olympics.

For African Americans, major-league teams were off limits. But black athletes were often able to demonstrate their abilities in individual sports. By rising to the top of their games, athletes like Jesse Owens and boxer Joe Louis helped set the stage for the integration of team sports.

The son of an Alabama sharecropper, Louis stormed onto the boxing scene, leaving a trail of victories behind him. He became a hero, inspiring many black youths. In 1937 Louis knocked out champion James Braddock in the eighth round to become the second black man to win a heavyweight championship (Jack Johnson was the first in 1908). He retired in 1949,

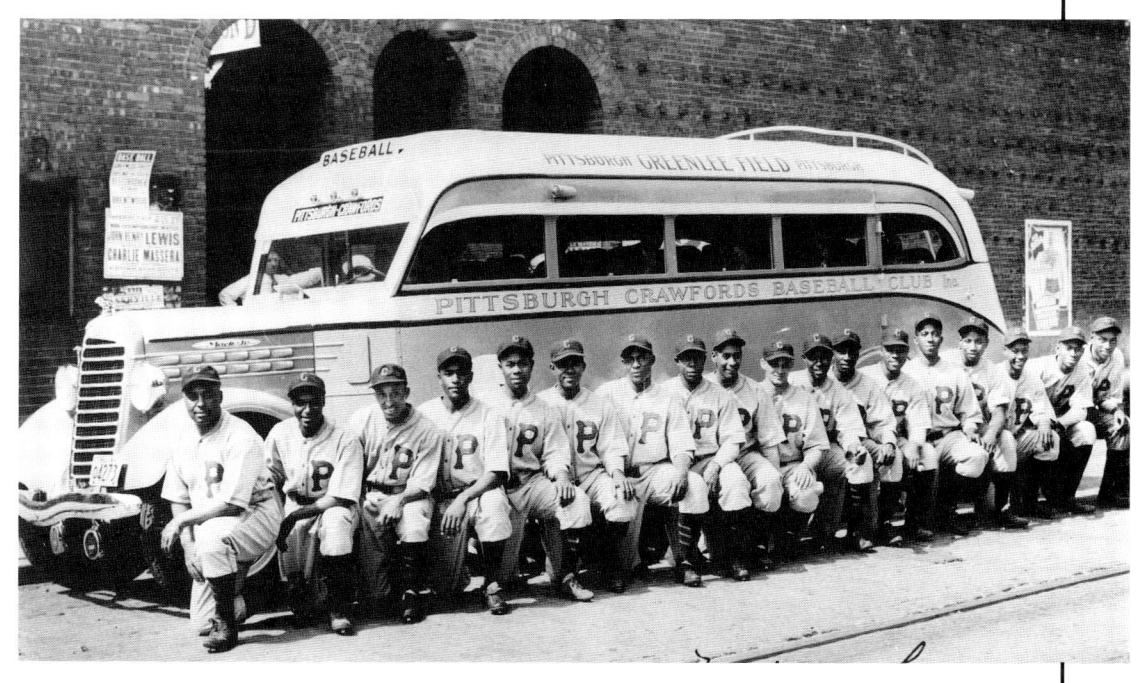

On the road with the Pittsburgh Crawfords of the Negro National League

A LEVEL PLAYING FIELD

with a career record of 62 fights, 52 knockout wins, 9 wins by decision, and one defeat. Louis was an exceptional fighter, but he was also an exemplary citizen who served in the army for two years during World War II. He won the hearts of many Americans, black and white, and opened the doors for other black athletes.

World War II changed America. As soldiers returned from the battlefields, they found a country ripe for change. Black veterans

Jim Thorpe

who had risked their lives overseas questioned discrimination and segregation at home. The civil rights movement was just gaining momentum, and black voting power was increasing. The U. S. government passed several anti-discrimination measures that helped minorities get jobs and better schooling.

For years, baseball had resisted integration, even with the rise and success of the Negro leagues. The all-black teams in those leagues had shown major-league team owners that black athletes could excel in the game of baseball and draw large crowds. Still, no team was willing to risk being the first to sign a black player.

Then, in 1945, Albert "Happy" Chandler became commissioner of the major leagues. He reasoned that if black men could fight for their country in World War II, they were good enough to play in the majors. He was willing to bring black players into the major leagues.

Baseball's racial experiment began that year when Jackie Robinson joined the Brooklyn Dodgers' farm club, the Montreal Royals. Baseball officials watched with great attention to see how Robinson would fare on a Canadian

Joe Louis was a hero to black and white youngsters.

team before daring to sign him on an American one. Robinson played second base and racked up statistics of a remarkable rookie season. His .349 batting average led the International League. He also led the league with his 113 runs scored and .985 fielding average. Robinson's debut in Montreal was just a warm-up.

On April 9, 1947, Dodgers president Branch Rickey announced that his team would sign Robinson. The announcement was greeted with pride, skepticism, and confusion. The black community was thrilled with Robinson's achievement, though black people were warned not to show too much enthusiasm toward Robinson. Black churches, newspapers, and leaders told fans to tone down their emotion: If they got too excited, they might scare away white fans or team owners and ruin Robinson's chances for staying in the majors. And if Robinson failed, baseball would

Jackie Robinson

be reluctant to sign another black player. Some skeptics believed that fewer people would attend baseball games because of Robinson and the other black players who were sure to follow. But many others believed that Robinson's contract was the first of many for black ballplayers.

The Negro leagues had other players who were arguably better than Robinson. But Rickey had chosen Robinson for a reason. Rickey knew that whoever became the first black athlete in organized ball in the 20th century would have to go through many hardships. He was looking for someone who had the strength to withstand prejudice and not fight back. He settled on Robinson because, aside from being a good athlete, Robinson was a model citizen. He was college-educated, had served in the army, had a solid marriage, and had shown that he could endure and rise above racial intolerance.

In the following years of his career, Robinson proved himself repeatedly. He ended his career with a lifetime .311 batting average. Along the way, he tolerated racial abuse at every turn. He persevered, even though the mental toll of enduring prejudice almost cost him a nervous breakdown. He offered hope for black people throughout the country.

A CHANCE TO PLAY

Many black players hoped that bringing Jackie Robinson into the major leagues would unleash a flood of black players into professional sports. They hoped that whole teams of blacks would be allowed into the big leagues. Instead, they had to settle for a trickle—integration would happen one person at a time.

The 1950s brought some of the game's greatest black players to the diamond. In 1954 Henry "Hank" Aaron joined the Milwaukee Braves, and after only three years, his talent as a slugger became obvious. His .328 batting average led the National League. Aaron and other black baseball players in this era felt lucky just to be a part of the game, and they played hard to stay on their teams. They endured poor treatment and racial taunts out of their love for the game. For instance, while hotels in rival cities welcomed white players, African Americans were often turned away and forced to search for accommodations in black neighborhoods.

THE NEGRO LEAGUES

In 1872 Bud Fowler became the first black player in professional baseball when he joined a minor-league team. Many black players followed his lead, and soon they formed a professional team, the Cuban Giants. As black players and teams became more common, many people thought that African Americans eventually would join the major leagues. But white players weren't ready to accept the change. That became clear in 1887 when Adrian "Cap" Anson, captain of the Chicago White Stockings, chose to leave the ball field rather than play against a team with a black pitcher.

In the early 1900s, independent black teams cropped up throughout the country. Many played against white teams and often showed they could outperform major leaguers. Tremendous changes occurred after World War I. In 1920 pitching star Andrew "Rube" Foster and a group of team owners created the Negro National League, made up of black teams in the Midwest. The new league brought organization to the teams and security for players. Games could be played according to a fixed schedule, and players received regular paychecks. Shortly afterward, a rival league—the Eastern Colored League—was created, made up of teams from the East Coast.

Life wasn't easy for the players, and they were never paid well. Willie Grace recalls playing for the Cleveland Buckeyes in the early 1940s: "I remember being in Mansfield, Ohio, right out of Cleveland. We played a twilight game, and we drove off to find some place to eat. We saw a cafe, but the owner saw us crossing the street, and he closed the place up . . . . We had some fine, fine ballplayers. The last four or five years of the Negro leagues, we had the best ballplayers in the world, and we didn't even know it."[1]

In the 1940s, many white baseball players left the major leagues to fight in World War II, and there was talk of allowing black players to try out for the majors. Black teams had proved they could draw crowds. In 1933, in Chicago's Comiskey Park, 40,000 fans had shown up to watch an All-Star game between the best talent from the eastern and midwestern leagues. During the war years, Negro league teams saw a rise in profits, as wartime crowds flocked to their games.

After the war, the major leagues signed Jackie Robinson. Soon, many major-league teams were looking to the Negro leagues for talent. A new era of integrated baseball began. But another era ended. As more black players moved into the big leagues in the 1950s, the Negro leagues faded away.

The 1921 Detroit Stars

A LEVEL PLAYING FIELD

As white players demanded higher salaries in the 1950s, baseball teams signed more and more black players, who were just as talented and would accept less pay. The idea of negotiating salaries was foreign to many African Americans, who traditionally had been confined to low-paying jobs. More important than pay, black players just wanted to show that they deserved a place on the field. Desegregation occurred gradually in baseball, with the Boston Red Sox becoming the last team to integrate in 1959.

Desegregation occurred just as slowly in other leagues. In 1950 the first black players signed with the National Basketball Association. Chuck Cooper joined the Boston Celtics, Earl Lloyd joined the Washington Capitols, and Nathaniel Clifton joined the New York Knickerbockers. Nine years later, the St. Louis Hawks became the last team in the NBA to sign a black player.

Kansas versus Nebraska, 1937. Neither college nor professional basketball teams accepted black players until the 1950s. Many college teams resisted integration well into the 1960s.

A BASKETBALL TRADITION

The 1930–31 Globetrotters and their manager (far left)

Before basketball teams integrated, black players already had established a tradition in the sport. Since the early 1920s, the Harlem Globetrotters had been playing against white teams. The Globetrotters featured some of the best black players in the country, and the team became famous for its style and superior playing ability. The Globetrotters never belonged to a league.

About the time that African Americans were first allowed into the Basketball Association of America, in 1946, the Globetrotters shifted their focus. They changed from a serious basketball team into an entertainment group, known for their antics and comic routines. The Globetrotters are often admired for their talent, but sometimes criticized for perpetuating stereotypes of black athletes, always playing tricks and fooling other players.

A LEVEL PLAYING FIELD

A force and a pioneer in football—Jim Brown

In 1946 Kenny Washington and Woody Strode signed with the Los Angeles Rams of the National Football League. The All-American Football Conference was formed the same year. Marion Motley and Bill Willis, who played for the Cleveland Browns, were the first black players in that league.

Seventeen years would pass before every American football team was integrated. Those tough years in which black athletes were striving to make a mark produced some of the sport's greatest performers, such as the Cleveland Browns' Jim Brown. Brown started setting records in his rookie year, leading the league in rushing. He kept that title eight out of the nine years of his career, which ended in 1965. He dominated the offense, carrying the ball 12,312 yards and scoring 126 touchdowns.

FRONT RUNNER

While Jackie Robinson was playing his first year in major league baseball, Althea Gibson of Harlem, New York, was creating a place for black athletes in the exclusive white tennis world. Her career gained speed in 1948, when she won the national Negro singles championship. Gibson defended that title for nine years and went on to make history on the American and international tennis scenes.

In 1950 Gibson became the first African American to play in the United States National Championships (now the U.S. Open). In 1956 she won the French Open. In 1957 she proved that she was the best female tennis player in the world. She won the coveted singles title at both Wimbledon (the English national championship) and the U.S. National Championships. In 1958 she defended both titles.

After Gibson's tennis career ended, she joined the Ladies Professional Golf Association tour and served as athletic commissioner of New Jersey. She also devoted her time to bringing tennis to inner-city youths, ensuring that the legacy of minorities in tennis would live on.

Cassius Clay, later known as Muhammad Ali, was famous for more than just boxing. He was active in civil rights and the antiwar movement.

CHANGING THE RULES

By the 1960s, minority athletes had established a place in professional sports. The issue was no longer whether they should be allowed to play but how they would be treated. The 1960s was a decade of social upheaval, with the civil rights movement at home and the Vietnam War abroad. The United States was redefining itself, and changes in sports were inevitable. Black athletes became more assertive—they were no longer willing to endure the pain of injustice quietly. Athletes took public stands, bringing their issues to international attention. Their cries were heard throughout the world.

Just as Joe Louis had done more than 20 years earlier, a boxer named Cassius Clay changed the world of boxing as well as the status of black athletes. In 1960 Clay won the light-heavyweight gold medal at the Olympic Games. Four years later, he defeated Sonny Liston to begin a long career as heavyweight champion, losing and regaining the title two times before retiring in 1980.

Clay was a different type of boxer. He was known for his graceful boxing style and his witty self-assurance. But he became

Ali spoke publicly and forcefully against the Vietnam War.

controversial for his politics rather than his boxing. After his fight with Liston, he announced his membership in the Nation of Islam, a Muslim group that promoted separation of the races. He took the Muslim name Muhammad Ali, arguing that Cassius Clay was a "slave name." Three years later, Ali refused to be drafted into the U.S. Army because his religion didn't condone fighting in war. He was convicted of violating draft laws and was sentenced to five years in prison and a $10,000 fine. His attorneys appealed the sentence, and Ali remained free on $5,000 bond. But because he had refused to be drafted, the World Boxing Association stripped him of his title. That move infuriated many African Americans, who thought that the decision was racially motivated. They argued that a white Quaker who espoused pacifism wouldn't have received the maximum sentence, as Ali had.

THE 1968 OLYMPICS—ATHLETES TAKE A STAND

Tommie Smith and John Carlos were on the medal stand. The scene was the 1968 Olympic Games in Mexico City. Smith had just won the gold medal in the 200-meter dash; Carlos, the bronze. As the U.S. national anthem played, Smith and Carlos bowed their heads and raised their gloved fists to the sky, a symbol of black power.

The medalists' gesture represented the struggle of black people in the United States. Smith and Carlos wore black stockings and no shoes to signify black poverty. They wore black scarves to represent the lynchings of black people. Their fists stood for black unity and power. Australian sprinter Peter Norman, who had won the silver medal, joined in the protest, wearing a button of the Olympic Project for Human Rights, a group that had called for black athletes to boycott the 1968 Games.

Smith and Carlos's gesture infuriated Olympic officials. The two sprinters were suspended from the U.S. Olympic team and thrown out of the Olympic village.

Other black athletes responded to the protest athletically and politically. Some athletes who had

Smith (left) and Carlos

intended to make a gesture on the medal stand did not, though they set world records that stood for years. Long jumper Bob Beamon leaped 29 feet, 2½ inches, breaking the world record by almost 2 feet. Wyomia Tyus defended her 100-meter title set at the 1964 Olympics, becoming the first woman to win that event twice. She dedicated her medal to Smith and Carlos. Overall, the African Americans on the U.S. Olympic team that year won 10 gold medals and set 7 world records. The 1968 Games was one of the most memorable displays of black athletic talent.

Why did black athletes win so many medals that year? Some say the world records and medals were the athletes' way of speaking out. Frustrated with racial inequality in the United States, the athletes translated their anger and yearning for civil rights into strength and speed.

Black athletes almost hadn't attended the 1968 Olympics. A movement to boycott the Games had gathered momentum in the months before. The debate reached a boiling point as the Games approached, and black athletes were divided as to whether or not to attend. Harry Edwards, then a professor at San Jose State University, spurred the movement, encouraging black athletes to use the only tool they had—their physical talent—to make a statement against segregation and discrimination. "If they won't rent to us, why should we run or play for them?" Edwards argued.[2]

Criticism came from both sides. "I deplore the use of the Olympic Games for political aggrandizement," Jesse Owens said.[3] But the boycott movement gained speed, winning the support of black leaders such as Dr. Martin Luther King Jr. and Jackie Robinson. Black athletes were encouraged to use their fame, their moment in the international spotlight, for a greater cause.

Still, the athletes were divided. Some supported the boycott; others considered it their duty to represent their country at the Games. In the end, the athletes decided not to boycott the Olympics, choosing to make a statement when they reached Mexico City. The protest began when Jim Hines, after setting a world record in the 100-meter race, avoided shaking hands with International Olympic Committee president Avery Brundage. The protest culminated in Smith and Carlos's gesture on the medal stand.

Throughout his career, Ali spoke out strongly against racial oppression. Other black athletes were less visible and vocal than Ali, but they were also making an impact. In basketball during this era, two greats emerged: Wilt Chamberlain and Bill Russell. One of basketball's all-time leading scorers, Chamberlain once racked up 100 points in a game. At 7 feet, 1 inch, he was arguably one of the greatest offensive threats in the sport.

By the time Russell came upon the scene, color barriers in basketball had come down, but the league had yet to have a black coach. In 1966, after a stellar playing career, Russell became the first black coach in the NBA, replacing Red Auerbach of the Boston Celtics.

During the Chamberlain and Russell era, pro basketball went through significant changes. Black athletes gained more visibility through television coverage of the games. As the quality of play improved, the popularity of the sport increased, and players were paid more. By the end of the decade, black athletes had become a dominant presence in basketball: 58 percent of the NBA roster was black, and 54 percent of the rival American Basketball Association's roster was black.

Though black athletes were moving into professional sports at a greater rate than ever, they were only allowed to play certain positions. Sports sociologist Harry Edwards calls this "stacking," the practice of putting black players in positions that don't require much thinking. Black players were labeled as less intelligent than their white teammates and were seldom allowed to be quarterbacks, pitchers, or catchers.

This phenomenon became most apparent in baseball in the 1960s. The percentage of black players in baseball far exceeded the percentage of black people in the United States. But black players were only occupying certain positions. Most played in the outfield or at first or second base. Blacks in "thinking" positions—pitcher, catcher, shortstop, and third base—were rare. The ratio of black outfielders to black pitchers was 5.6 to 1 in 1960, and by 1970 the ratio had worsened to 6.7 to 1.

THE BIG PAYOFF

By the 1970s, minorities were a dominant force in professional sports. Their talents often brought

RECORD BREAKER

In 1974, 20 years after Hank Aaron became part of the Braves lineup, he broke Babe Ruth's home run record, one of the greatest achievements in the game. Many white fans were upset that a black player dared to break the record of one of baseball's greats, who was white. As Aaron approached his 715th home run, which broke the record, he received death threats and hate mail filled with racial slurs.

A LEVEL PLAYING FIELD

them fame, but not a high salary. Most sports teams operated under a reserve clause, which meant that the first team that signed a player controlled his career. Players essentially were the property of their teams and could be traded or sold. Under this system, salaries were relatively low. Bargaining for salaries was uncommon. In the 1970s, the average salary in major-league baseball was $29,303 (compared with $1.2 million in 1994). Football players

Minority athletes no longer take a back seat to white players. Stars like Randall Cunningham (left) and Bobby Bonilla (above) are well paid and highly respected.

made an average of $23,000, and basketball players earned an average of $43,000. On average, African-American players earned less than whites.

The reserve system crumbled in the 1970s. Athletes became free agents, able to negotiate their contracts and salaries. Pay for athletes in general skyrocketed. Minority athletes gained status and wealth. But black players still usually earned less than their white teammates.

By the late 1980s, the situation had changed. Salaries for black football players had increased and were larger than any others in the NFL, according to a *USA Today* survey. And black quarterbacks earned more than white quarterbacks—largely because the black quarterbacks of that time, namely Randall Cunningham, Doug Williams, and Warren Moon, were extremely successful. The situation was different in baseball, though, where most white players earned higher salaries than minorities. Only pitchers had similar salaries, regardless of race.

In the 1990s, performance more than race determines a player's salary. According to a 1991 *Sports Illustrated* survey, most minority players believe they can expect equal treatment in terms of salaries. Indeed, some of the highest paid players in pro sports are minorities. In 1992 the New York Mets' Bobby Bonilla, a Hispanic ballplayer, was the highest paid player in baseball.

While there's no disputing that superstars such as Bonilla are paid generously, salaries for average minority players may lag behind. "While the superstar Hispanic player is compensated on a par with comparable non-Hispanic players, the average Hispanic player is not compensated equally," remarks Jaime Torres, an agent for athletes.[4]

Despite some inequities, many of today's minority athletes enjoy privileges from money and fame. The playing field has become more level, but racism, discrimination, and stereotypes have not disappeared from the world of sports.

CHAPTER TWO

TYPECASTING

When Jewish men dominated basketball in the 1920s and 1930s, the media looked for ways to explain why Jewish athletes excelled in the game. Rather than acknowledging the players' talents, reporters resorted to stereotypes. A 1933 *New York Daily News* article said, "Jewish players seem to take naturally to the game. Perhaps this is because the Jew is a natural gambler and will take chances. Perhaps it is because he devotes himself more closely to a problem than others will."[1]

When black athletes became more prominent in sports, the media again looked for reasons beyond hard work and training that black athletes played football, basketball, and baseball so well. To show that black athletes were physically different than white athletes, reporters came up with ideas that sounded scientific but had no basis in fact.

A 1971 *Sports Illustrated* article declared that blacks had more tendons than whites. That gave them a "double-jointedness" and "looseness" that enabled them to dominate in sports, the article said. It continued, "Perhaps be-cause of the greater density of their bone and muscle, the distribution of their fat and their smaller lung capacity, certain blacks have difficulty learning to swim. Such individuals are what swimming coaches call 'sinkers.'"[2]

The article enraged black athletes. "All the racial upheaval of the 1960s had taught *Sports Illustrated* was that it's OK to be racist as long as you try to sound like a doctor," said Celtics coach Bill Russell.[3]

Racial stereotypes have persisted into the 1980s and 1990s. Al Campanis, vice president of player personnel for the Los Angeles Dodgers remarked that fewer blacks became swimmers because African Americans couldn't float as well as whites. Baltimore Orioles scout Fred Uhlman Sr. was quoted as saying: "A lot of Mexicans have bad foot speed. It's a genetic-type thing. They have a different body type. Most all have good hands and good rhythm. That's why they dance so well. Rhythm is important in baseball; it means agility."[4] The Orioles reprimanded Uhlman for his remarks.

Some racial stereotyping is more subtle. Studies have shown that broadcasters more often refer to white athletes by their last names and minority athletes by their first names, showing minorities less respect and making them seem less serious and less mature than their white teammates.

Athletes continue to fight stereotypes in basketball and other sports.

In addition, black athletes are most often described by the media in terms of athleticism and strength. White players are described in terms of intelligence, leadership, and motivation. At a game between Duke University and the University of Maryland, a CBS broadcaster described a white player's pass this way: "There is patience. There is the artist at work, waiting for people to uncover, sensing the defense was looking at him entirely." When the sportscaster was describing the all-black Maryland team, he used words such as "mobile," "great leaping ability," and "jumped out of the building."[5]

STACKING THE DECK

J. R. Richard, a black pitcher for the Houston Astros, was having his best season in 1980. He had 119 strikeouts and led the league with a 1.80 earned run average. When he complained that he felt a numbness in his arm, the media called him lazy. Some reporters accused him of taking drugs. His ability to play diminished. Soon, he couldn't last more than a few innings. When doctors examined him, they found a blood clot. But Richard was still allowed to pitch. When he was working out for the first time after the examination, he had a stroke, which he barely survived.

Black teammates were angry at Richard's treatment. They said a white pitcher with a similar health condition wouldn't have been called lazy or faced accusations of drug use—criticisms that reflect stereotypes and prejudices about African Americans.

Another racial stereotype casts African Americans as less intelligent than their white teammates. This stereotype can lead to stacking, the segregation of players by position. Statistics show that black players are more often assigned to positions that require running ability or strength. White players more often play positions that require intelligence, leadership, and knowledge of strategy.

Northeastern University's Racial Report Card, a yearly analysis of racial issues in professional sports, shows that stacking is still a problem in football and baseball. (Stacking isn't really an issue in basketball because so many players are black.) In 1992 only 6 percent of black football players were quarterbacks, even though 68 percent of the players in the NFL were black, 30 percent were white, and 2 percent were of other races.

In baseball the figures were not much better. In 1993 only 5 percent of black players and 12 percent of Latino players were pitchers. Most black players occupied outfield positions, but 50 percent of Latino players occupied the key position of shortstop.

WAR WHOOPS AND TOMAHAWK CHOPS

Racial stereotypes in sports go beyond the playing field—into the stands and even the souvenir booth. Imagine being at a New Orleans Saints football game. When a player scores a touchdown, all the fans start waving crucifixes and chanting Hail Marys. Would Christian fans be offended? Of course.

That's what Native Americans say it feels like when they see crowds yelling war whoops and doing tomahawk chops at Washington Redskins football games or Atlanta Braves baseball games.

Fans like these make a mockery of Native American symbols, many critics say.

A LEVEL PLAYING FIELD

Some fans argue that names such as the Chiefs and the Braves pay tribute to American Indians.

They say using Indian mascots for sports teams promotes stereotypes of Native Americans and mocks their rituals and way of life. Native American people have been fighting for years to bring an end to the behavior they call racist.

No one would think of calling a team the "slaves" and using a black person as a mascot. That practice would be offensive and disrespectful to African Americans. Native Americans say they're not treated with the same respect. The name "Redskin" has a painful meaning for Native Americans. It calls to mind crimes committed against Indians during the 19th century, when white bounty hunters would bring in "red skins" for rewards.

Many student and professional teams have Indian mascots. At Florida State games, a student dressed as a Seminole Indian wears a headdress onto the field and plants a burning spear in the ground. Among the souvenirs sold to Kansas City Chiefs fans are war paint and Indian costumes. Native Americans say these mascots and souvenirs are racist.

"It hurts," says Roger Head, the head of the Minnesota Indian Affairs Council. "It's not a true depiction of the Indian people. When we see these folks dressed as Indians and wearing war paint, the stereotypes of Indians come out. They wear headdresses, which are very spiritual in nature, very ceremonial."[6]

In some Native American cultures, the eagle feather signifies respect between a father and his son. A headdress full of eagle feathers represents years of life experience and symbolizes the respect and affection a man has earned throughout his lifetime. Native Americans see fans wearing headdresses as a mockery of

Clyde Bellecourt, director of the American Indian Movement, leads a demonstraton against the Washington Redskins at the 1992 Super Bowl.

Native American traditions and symbols.

In the past few years, some teams have tried to change their names and mascots. A few teams have succeeded, but others have met a lot of controversy. Many fans and team members say they're *honoring* Native Americans when they put on war paint and wear headdresses. They say they're proud to wear these emblems—they represent bravery in battle, school spirit, and team traditions.

Opponents argue that these are not traditions worth keeping, especially if they hurt Native American people. The most successful efforts to change mascots have come from schools. Stanford and Marquette universities dropped

Despite protests, no major-league sports team has dropped its Indian name and mascot.

their Indian mascots after students protested. High schools around the country have also changed their team names and mascots.

Despite protests staged at World Series games and the Super Bowl, professional teams have done little to address Native Americans' concerns. More money is at stake for professional than for high school teams, and that's why they won't change their names, some people say. Team owners must consider the moral side of the issue. But the financial side may be what drives a decision. A team could risk losing fans or money by changing its mascot.

The team owners say that "even if they did decide to change the name, it would take them several years to do that because of marketing," says Clyde Bellecourt, national director of the American Indian Movement. "I don't believe that. I believe that if they changed the name tomorrow, any merchandise they had left probably would triple in price."[7]

The American Indian Movement has been working since its founding in 1968 to end the use of Native American mascots. Recently, some help has come from the media. In 1992 the Portland *Oregonian* announced it would not print offensive team names. Instead, the newspaper would refer to teams such as the Washington Redskins as the Washington football team. The Minneapolis *Star Tribune* adopted a similar policy in the winter of 1994.

"These names tend to perpetuate stereotypes that damage the dignity and self-respect of many people in our society," *Oregonian* editor William Hilliard said, "and this harm far transcends any innocent entertainment or promotional value these names may have."[8]

Professional teams have not been swayed by the media or protests. No major-league team has abandoned an Indian name. But as long as the sporting community continues to promote stereotypes—of Native Americans, blacks, Hispanics, or any other group—the voices of protest will not die down.

A LEVEL PLAYING FIELD

Art Shell is one of just two black head coaches in the NFL.

CHAPTER THREE

WHO'S IN CHARGE?

In November 1991, when Charles Barkley played for the Philadelphia 76ers, he shocked the sports world when he said that the 76ers wouldn't trade their one white player because management would be scared to have an all-black team. Barkley was accusing the 76ers of sticking to a quota system, allowing only a certain number of black athletes on the team.

All professional teams deny that they use quotas, but many players say there's an unspoken effort to limit the number of minority players in professional sports. Unlike businesses or universities, which use quotas as a way to bring more minorities to an organization, quota systems in sports ensure that each team has a certain amount of *white* players. According to a 1991 *Sports Illustrated* survey, 58 percent of black athletes and 18 percent of white athletes believed teams used racial quotas in hiring decisions.

In the 1980s, Cleveland Cavaliers owner Ted Stepien traded a number of outstanding black players for whites who did not have comparable talents. He said that the Cavaliers had too

A LEVEL PLAYING FIELD

many black ballplayers—ten of eleven. He thought a racially balanced team would be more popular.

The idea that black athletes wouldn't draw white fans fed this perception. A 1980 survey of Philadelphia residents suggested that this notion might be true. At the time, the 76ers were top ranked in the NBA, led by Dr. J—Julius Erving. Still, ticket sales were 55 percent of what they could have been. Meanwhile, the Boston Celtics, a team that had white stars such as Larry Bird, were selling out most of their games.

A LOOK AT THE NUMBERS

Though the sports world is often criticized for using quotas and unfair hiring practices, sports surpasses American society in the treatment of minorities. In the 1990s, the income gap between

Do white basketball stars like former Boston Celtic Larry Bird bring more fans to the arena than black stars do?

minorities and whites widened. According to U.S. census data, minorities were up to three times more likely to be poor than white Americans. In 1988, 31.3 percent of the African-American population and 26.7 of Hispanics lived at poverty level, compared with 10.1 percent of the white population.

In this context, sports fares well. The sports world has welcomed many minorities into its exclusive arena. Of the three big professional leagues, the NBA has the highest percentage of minority players. According to Northeastern University's 1993 Racial Report Card, 77 percent of NBA players are black, and 68 percent in the NFL are black.

The number of black players in major-league baseball has decreased over several years, reaching 16 percent in 1993. But the number of Hispanic players in baseball has *increased* to 16 percent. Though major-league baseball has been criticized for its lack of minority players, the percentage of minorities in the league well exceeds the percentage of minorities in the American population.

Despite these statistics, racial barriers persist in major-league sports. Many minority players feel they must play better than their white teammates just to stay on the team. San Diego Padres reliever Rich Rodriguez told *Sports Illustrated*, "Most minorities that make it to the majors tend to be the superstar-type player. You rarely see a minority with average talent go up to the majors.... [Yet] there are a lot of white guys in the majors who are hanging on to their jobs and should be gone by now."[1]

And though some minority athletes reach the big league playing field, few call the shots. In the professional ranks, many minorities are locked out of key positions due to stacking. Many more are unable to land a management or coaching job when their playing days are over.

Charles Barkley accuses team owners of racism.

SIDELINED

As the first black player in the American League, right fielder Larry Doby had a lot to prove. Just like Jackie Robinson in the

National League, he was a pioneer and carried the hopes of future black generations. He knew what it took to win, batting a .301 average in 1948.

In 1968 Doby told *Sports Illustrated:* "Baseball has done a lot for the Negro, but the Negro has done more for baseball. Black players have meant gold for baseball owners. I drew a lot of people into Cleveland in those days. I was surprised about two things. Surprised I ever got a chance to play in the big leagues and more surprised I didn't get a chance to stay in [as a coach] when I was through playing. After all, I was a pioneer. It doesn't make sense to me that an insurance company would give me the chance to prove I could handle a job, but baseball wouldn't let me try."[2]

Shortly after his comments appeared in the magazine, Doby was hired as a coach for Cleveland. But his remarks showed the frustration that many minority players feel when they are overlooked for coaching or management positions.

Like Doby, pitcher Earl Wilson protested the lack of opportunities for African Americans in sports management: "People say wait five or ten years and it will happen," Wilson told *Sports Illustrated* in 1968. "Well, man, I can't wait. It has to happen now."[3]

But more than 20 years after Doby and Wilson made their remarks, little has changed. On the ABC television show *Nightline* in 1987, Al Campanis said that African Americans "may not have some of the necessities to be, let's say, a field manager, or perhaps a general manager." In 1988 CBS broadcaster Jimmy "the Greek" Snyder made racist remarks on the physical differences between black and white athletes. He also said that black coaches would be a threat to the white power structure in professional sports. In 1993 Cincinnati Reds owner Marge Schott reportedly said that she'd "rather have a trained monkey working for me than a nigger."[4]

These remarks provoked outrage, highlighting racism in sports and the lack of minorities in the front office. But they did little to spur change. Beyond the playing field, few minorities hold positions of authority. Managers, administrators, team doctors, and coaches make up a mostly white roster.

Frank Robinson was the first black manager in the major leagues. His signing with the

Cleveland Indians in 1974 as a manager was as revolutionary as Jackie Robinson's joining the major leagues. But hiring practices since Frank Robinson's signing have not gone much beyond the employment of a token number of minorities.

"Based on the record of the organizations, I don't think that we have been able to break through yet," says Frank Robinson. "And I think that is evidenced by how many major league managers have been hired since [Campanis's remarks] and how few minorities have been given a chance."[5]

THE OLD BOYS' NETWORK

To be sure, there are plenty of minority candidates for management jobs. Players, for example, are a natural choice for coaching and front-office positions. Their experience on the playing field gives them insight into the psychology and nature of the game.

Marge Schott, owner of the Cincinnati Reds baseball team, drew heavy criticism for making racist remarks.

RACIAL REPORT CARD

Minority head coaches and managers in the major leagues:

	NBA	NFL	MLB
1988–89			
White	80% (20)	100% (28)	96% (27)
Black	20% (5)	(0)	4% (1)
1989–90			
White	78% (21)	96% (27)	96% (27)
Black	22% (6)	4% (1)	4% (1)
1990–91			
White	78% (21)	96% (27)	93% (26)
Black	22% (6)	4% (1)	7% (2)
1991–92			
White	93% (25)	93% (26)	89% (25)
Black	7% (2)	7% (2)	7% (2)
Hispanic	(0)	(0)	4% (1)
1992–93			
White	74% (20)	89% (25)	79% (22)
Black	26% (7)	7% (2)	14% (4)
Hispanic	(0)	4% (1)	7% (2)
1993–94			
White	80% (20)	89% (25)	82% (25)
Black	20% (5)	7% (2)	14% (4)
Hispanic	(0)	4% (1)	4% (1)

Radio and television announcers, 1994:

	NBA	NFL	MLB
White	80%	85%	83%
Black	12%	2%	5%
Hispanic	7%	13%	12%

Source: Racial Report Card, a yearly analysis of racial issues in football, basketball, and baseball. Northeastern University's Center for the Study of Sport in Society.

But minority candidates tell story after story of being passed up for coaching jobs. In 1991 seven managerial vacancies opened in major-league baseball. All positions were filled by white candidates. None had experience in the major leagues, a qualification often cited as a reason for not hiring minorities.

Former Bengal player Reggie Williams, a Dartmouth University graduate and former Cincinnati City Council member, had trouble breaking into NFL management. "The Cincinnati Bengals have a policy that you have to learn elsewhere. They have no one in the front office who is a person of color," he told the *New York Times* in 1992.[6] The NFL wouldn't hire Williams, who later landed a general manager position with the New York/New Jersey Knights in the World Football League.

Meanwhile, white coaches and managers establish themselves as familiar faces and are hired and rehired. In 17 years, white baseball manager John McNamara moved among six teams and ended up with an overall losing record. Cincinnati's Pete Rose had a manager job waiting for him when he walked off the baseball diamond. White "managers are hired and fired every day," noted baseball great Hank Aaron. "That manager goes somewhere else and gets the same type job. That's the thing that bothers me."[7]

To play on a pro team, an athlete usually follows a specific track. It often begins early on, with youth league, junior high, and high school teams. Some athletes, especially baseball players, join professional teams right after high

Though most NBA players are black, most NBA coaches are white. John Lucas is one of the exceptions.

school. Others go on to the college level. Professional basketball and football teams fill their rosters from the top college teams.

On the management level, the path to a head coaching or general manager position is less clear-cut. Getting a job depends not only on experience and talent but also on networking and business contacts. The Cincinnati Bengals' David Shula, son of the NFL's most successful coach, Don Shula, is the youngest coach in league history. He was named head coach of the Bengals in 1992 at age 33. Having a heavyweight and influential last name likely helped David Shula move up quickly and stay there, despite his team's losing streak.

Indeed, when it comes to hiring, those in charge—general managers, team presidents, and team owners—often choose job candidates from within the "old boys' network," an exclusive club of friends and colleagues, who are usually white. Many minorities say that the network is racist. Team owners say that's not true. Everyone on a team, from the players to the owner, wants the same thing: to win. Many people believe that team decision-makers don't consciously decide not to hire a minority coach. They try to choose the best-qualified person for a position, regardless of race.

Still, "when it comes time for . . . [picking] a managerial coach, it's who do you know, who your friends are, and a lot of times, that small network is white people, and so minorities don't always get a fair shake from the start," says Jeffrey Benedict, research assistant at Northeastern University's Center for the Study of Sport in Society.[8]

Teams may not have outright discriminatory hiring methods,

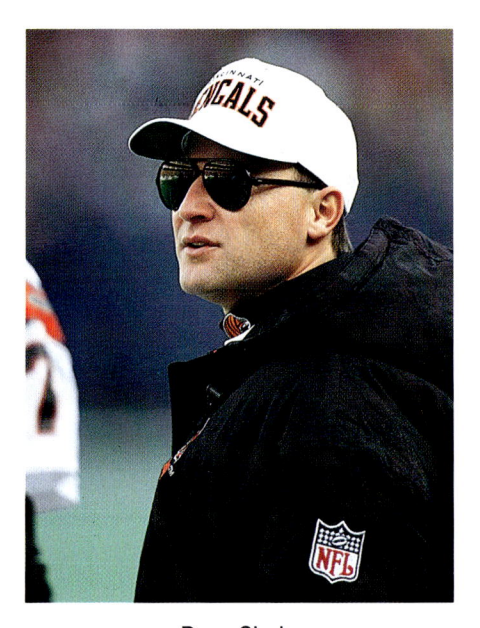

Dave Shula

SPORTS AND RACE   45

College athletes often play before an audience of white students and alumni.

but the numbers don't lie. College coaching staffs are mostly white. In 1991 only 30 of 290 Division I schools had black head coaches in basketball. Of 106 Division I football programs, only two had black head coaches, and baseball had none.

Black coaches are rare at mostly white schools, where most wealthy donors and fans are also white.

"Many presidents and athletic directors fear that they'll lose some of their grass-roots support if they hire a black coach," commented Arizona State University assistant head coach Frank Falks.[9]

Since the late 1980s, professional and college hiring practices have come under closer scrutiny. In 1987, 17 assistant basketball coaches formed the Black

Coaches Association to protest the lack of black head coaches. Working at mostly white universities, these coaches had seen their white peers work their way up to head coaching jobs, while the only opportunities for minorities were in recruiting positions.

Joining the movement for fair hiring practices is civil rights leader Jesse Jackson. He formed the Rainbow Commission for Fairness in Athletics. "The future of African Americans and Latin players . . . is almost absolute," Jackson explained. "Orlando Cepeda, Joe Morgan, Ernie Banks, Cesar Cedeno, Enos Cabell, Curt Flood, Bob Gibson, Reggie Jackson, John Roseboro, to name a few, have no place in baseball beyond their playing days."[10]

Much of the hiring momentum in the professional leagues is set by the leagues' commissioners. In 1945 Happy Chandler set the stage for Jackie Robinson's entry into major-league baseball. More recently Fay Vincent, baseball commissioner from 1989 to 1992, said that minority hiring is good for business: "Now in a world where non-white minorities are an increasing part of the American population, that means that baseball is selling itself primarily to a shrinking part of the market. To me, as a businessman, that's a losing proposition. And no one in baseball likes losing."[11]

ON CAMERA

The situation in sports broadcasting is much like the one in sports management—white people dominate top decision-making positions. Although some minorities occupy lower level posts in sportscasting and production, few move up to the higher level jobs of producer, director, or manager. Northeastern University's 1993 Racial Report Card noted that only 19 percent of NBA radio and television announcers, 14 percent of NFL announcers, and 17 percent of baseball announcers were minorities.

"I've seen a few [black] guys come but they don't stay," said Ken Edmundson, a black producer at NBC. "Where are these people going and why aren't they being promoted? It's racism . . . I'm glad to see what [play-by-play broadcaster and studio anchor] James Brown has done at CBS. He's getting a lot of good exposure and doing a good job. But who else? You get your quota and that's it. Who really cares? The

Sportscasting jobs usually go to whites, many former athletes say.

sponsors don't care and the public really doesn't care other than the government."[12]

TV networks often employ former athletes, many of color, to provide commentary during specific games. But because these athletes are highly visible, critics say, their appearance creates an illusion of equal opportunity in sportscasting. In broadcasting as on the playing field, the multiracial image on screen often masks a very different situation behind the camera.

CHAPTER FOUR

BEYOND THE PLAYING FIELD

When a first-round draft pick signs with a team, the question is not only which team, but also which endorsement contracts he will sign. Professional sports is big business; multimillion-dollar salaries are common. But endorsing products is even bigger business. Top athletes can double or triple their incomes, using their images to sell everything from athletic shoes to hamburgers. Endorsements ensure financial security in the sports world, where stars can rise and fall in a matter of seconds.

Television commercials can catapult little known or little noticed players to superstar status. Athletes who are praised for their physical skills might also become famous for their smiles and personalities. Because of endorsements, black athletes like Michael Jordan and Earvin "Magic" Johnson have broad appeal. They're heroes to people of all races. With this ability to "cross over" comes large paychecks and, some say, added responsibility. Many athletes are urged to speak out on racial issues because of their ability to appeal to large audiences.

WHITEWASHED

Companies haven't always been willing to hire black athletes as spokespeople. For many years, minorities were considered too risky—corporate America thought that consumers wouldn't trust a minority athlete. That's not to say that black athletes didn't appeal to white audiences. Track stars Jesse Owens and Wilma Rudolph and boxing legend Joe Louis had wide appeal. Though they had fans of all races, these athletes couldn't profit financially from their fame.

By the 1960s and 1970s, a few minority athletes had won endorsement contracts, although not the multimillion-dollar deals athletes get today. African-American tennis star Arthur Ashe was one of the pioneers. After a lot of hesitation, the Head sports equipment company created an Arthur Ashe model tennis racket. Golf legend Lee Trevino, a Mexican

Arthur Ashe in his tennis-playing days

American, also had success. Since his career began in 1965, Trevino has earned millions hawking products for companies such as Cadillac, Motorola, R. J. Reynolds, and Spalding.

But well into the 1980s, minority athletes had a harder time cashing in on their achievements than did white players. White quarterback Jim McMahon earned more than $1 million in endorsements after the Chicago Bears' Super Bowl victory in 1986. Phil Simms, the New York Giants quarterback who is also white, made more than $750,000 for the same achievement in 1987. But black quarterback Doug Williams, who led the Washington Redskins to victory in 1988, earned only $127,500 in endorsement money.

Advertisers "will almost immediately go to a white athlete," said Harry Edwards in 1988. "These aren't people who consider this kind of thing to be racist—[choosing a black athlete] just never crosses their mind."[1]

BASKETBALL BREAKTHROUGH

In 1985 the National Basketball Association was on the verge of bankruptcy and troubled with a reputation for having drug-addicted players. At the same time, the shoe company Nike was looking for a spokesperson. Nike gambled on an NBA rookie who had led North Carolina to a National Collegiate Athletic Association (NCAA) championship. The timing was perfect for Chicago Bull Michael Jordan, the NBA, and Oregon-based Nike.

Jordan breathed new life into the NBA, and the Nike ads cemented his popularity and propelled him to superstardom. Jordan had all the characteristics a company could want: He was an intelligent, outstanding athlete who lived a clean lifestyle, had a family, and projected an engaging personality. The one thing that made Jordan different from most of the corporate spokespeople who had preceded him was his race.

Nike launched a pair of shoes named Air Jordan and marketed the shoes in witty commercials directed by filmmaker Spike Lee. The success of Air Jordan and the appeal of Jordan as an athlete and spokesman revolutionized sports and advertising. His success as an endorser was so great that he went on to become a spokesman for non-sports products. By the time he retired from basketball in 1993,

SPORTS AND RACE 51

he was earning more than $30 million a year by endorsing products for Nike, McDonald's, Sara Lee, General Mills, Quaker Oats, and Wilson Sporting Goods.

The success of Nike's campaign with Jordan broke down barriers for other minority athletes. Advertisers, once afraid to use a spokesman from the mostly black NBA, flocked to it. After Michael Jordan retired in 1993, advertisers and

Young people look up to Michael Jordan. Companies hope that youths who want to "be like Mike" will buy the products he endorses.

52 ◼ A LEVEL PLAYING FIELD

Kristi Yamaguchi has star quality. But does she look too ethnic to appeal to American consumers?

fans wondered who in the NBA would be corporate America's next Michael Jordan. Immediately, Charles Barkley and Shaquille O'Neal stepped into the spotlight, snatching up endorsements because of their popularity and undeniable playing style.

WHO CASHES IN?

Olympic gold medalist Kristi Yamaguchi had an image problem. A fifth-generation Japanese American, she won her medal in figure skating in 1992, during a time of American resentment toward Japanese economic power. Shortly after the Olympics, *Business Week* reported: "Companies may be shying away from Yamaguchi because of her ethnic heritage. She was born in the U.S., as were her folks, but her surname and looks are Japanese."[2]

Four months after her victory in Albertville, France, Yamaguchi landed her first endorsement contract. Hoechst Celanese, a company that manufactures acetate fibers that are made into clothing, chose Yamaguchi as its spokeswoman. The ice skater's yearly income from endorsements is an estimated $300,000.

But her bronze-medal-winning teammate Nancy Kerrigan, who is white, raked in endorsements after the 1992 Games because of her all-American appeal. After the infamous attack on Kerrigan by the associates of skating rival Tonya Harding in 1994, Kerrigan soared to superstar status and won more than $11 million in endorsement deals.

But does the income difference between Yamaguchi and Kerrigan stem from racism? In the search for a spokesperson, advertisers say they seek top athletes who have charisma—something that differentiates them from the rest. There is no real formula for what makes a good endorser. Not all champions and not all athletes with intriguing personalities will get endorsements. Race doesn't enter into the picture, advertisers say. The business success of black basketball players in recent years seems to support this argument.

But some industry critics say that today's minority athletes must be *more* skilled, charming, and accomplished than white athletes to be attractive to corporate America and white consumers. And minority athletes who can transform their popularity into endorsement dollars sometimes fall victim to a different kind of racism.

Advertisers often portray black athletes as streetwise and tough. In an advertisement for Converse shoes, Magic Johnson appears in a slick leather jacket, looking intimidating as he poses on top of a Cadillac. The caption of the ad says, "Chillin'." The same company portrayed tennis star Jimmy Connors with his wife in a domestic setting. The caption of the Connors ad reads, "Heartthrob."

Advertisers say that these portrayals are designed to appeal to different audiences. But critics say such advertisements perpetuate racial stereotypes and fail to project positive images of African Americans.

Should a black athlete agree to appear in an advertisement that might project a racial stereotype? And just because a minority athlete is talented and popular, is he or she obligated to become a spokesperson for racial justice?

A ROLE MODEL'S ROLE

On April 29, 1992, the city of Los Angeles erupted. A jury had just given a verdict of innocent to four police officers who faced criminal charges in the beating of black motorist Rodney King. The nation was caught up in the drama of the trial, having seen the beating, which an amateur video cameraman had captured on tape. Images of white policemen attacking a black man stretched racial tensions to the breaking point. As news of the verdict spread through Los Angeles, tension turned into anger and frustration. Across the city, African Americans, angry with the injustice of the legal system, rioted.

That night, basketball and baseball games were scheduled in Los Angeles. But these events were canceled because they were to be held in facilities in riot-torn areas. The games came to a halt out of concern for the safety of fans and players.

Many athletes had grown up in neighborhoods similar to the ones where the riots occurred. These players could understand the anger and fear of the rioters. A few athletes, such as Los Angeles Clippers center Olden Polynice and former Cleveland Brown Jim Brown, headed into the heart of Los Angeles to help the region rebuild. But most didn't venture beyond their homes or hotel rooms. Though many athletes pleaded for a solution to the violence when reporters questioned them, few used their fame to work for change. Minority athletes were criticized for not doing more to help the riot-torn city. Critics said they had shirked the responsibility that comes with fame.

Athletes are part of everyday life, thanks to endorsements. Their fame is not limited to the world of sports. People who have never seen a basketball game can identify Michael Jordan because he appears in advertisements for hamburgers, hot dogs, lottery tickets, and sports drinks. And they know Orlando's Shaquille O'Neal from Pepsi advertisements.

Many people say that once these athletes sign a contract to endorse a product, they accept an unwritten responsibility. They must recognize that impressionable young people admire them, and many

Shaquille O'Neal of the Orlando Magic helps sell Pepsi on TV.

A LEVEL PLAYING FIELD

will want to imitate their actions. They become role models—that's the price of fame. For minority athletes, that price is even greater. They're expected to use their influence to fight racial injustice and to create opportunities for the next generation.

Some athletes don't want the burden. In a Nike TV commercial, Charles Barkley declares, "I am not a role model. I am not paid to be a role model. I am paid to wreak havoc on the basketball court. Parents should be role models. Just because I can dunk a basketball doesn't mean I should raise your kids."

ATHLETE OR ACTIVIST?

During the civil rights movement, the sports arena was seen as an avenue to help bring about social change; athletes were encouraged to use their fame as a tool in the fight for equality. At the 1968 Olympics, runners Tommie Smith and

Athletes are heroes and role models to young people of all races.

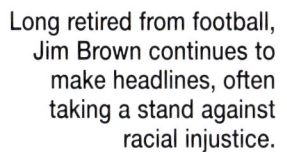

Long retired from football, Jim Brown continues to make headlines, often taking a stand against racial injustice.

John Carlos responded to that call to action, raising their fists on the medal stand as a symbol of black power. They took a tremendous risk: Carlos later said that while he was on the stand, he held his arm half-cocked, ready to defend himself. He thought he was sure to be killed for his act of defiance.

Smith and Carlos paid a price for speaking out. They were banished from the Olympic village in Mexico City. When they returned home to the United States, employers wouldn't hire them because they were perceived as troublemakers. Athletes like Smith and Carlos are rare. Making an imprint in the sports history books wasn't enough for them. They reached beyond the sheltered world of sports to touch a nation's conscience, changing people and the world around them.

Though today's minority athletes are far wealthier and treated much better than were their predecessors, many people say minority athletes still need to speak out. If athletes were more vocal, some say, they could use their influence to bring about change in sports and society. For example, a collective boycott by athletes would send a message to team owners about the need for more minorities in the front office.

But in the sports world today, money talks, athletes don't. They're part of a multimillion-dollar establishment. Today's athletes are more reserved, and many suspect that's because they don't want to put their contracts or endorsement dollars at stake. The risks of speaking out aren't as great for top athletes because they're so valuable to their teams and endorsers. But for marginal players, who are more easily replaced, the risks of speaking out on racial issues can have negative consequences.

A *New York Times* article told the story of Craig Hodges, an average player for the Chicago Bulls. One season, he spoke against racial injustice and publicly criticized teammate Michael Jordan for his silence on racial issues. "The poverty in this city is so hellish," Hodges said. "The reason the poverty continues is because brothers like [Jordan] . . . are extracted out of the city."[3] The Bulls dropped Hodges after the playoffs, and he couldn't get a tryout from another team in the NBA. Former Detroit Piston Isiah Thomas also has been vocal about racial issues, and many say his endorsement and salary potential suffered because of his openness.

To appeal to a mass audience, athletes in some sense must mute their racial identity and opinions. Arthur Ashe explained: "Michael [Jordan] was criticized for not getting involved in the last election when Harvey Gantt, a black candidate, was running against Senator Jesse Helms in Jordan's home state of North Carolina. But if you're going to be a genuine sports hero in this country, a [Babe] Ruth, [Joe] DiMaggio or [Arnold] Palmer, you have to keep your political views to yourself. Advertisers want somebody who's politically neutered. That's unspoken, but it's understood."[4]

MORE WORK AHEAD

It may be naive to think that athletes can help solve social problems. But their fame gives them the opportunity to make an impact. As long as racial inequities exist, athletes should use their stature to bring about change, many say. And black players are often reminded that they've only gotten their shot at fame and fortune because of pioneers like Hank Aaron. He endured many hardships because of his race and paved the way for the next generation.

The fact that some black athletes have become wealthy and famous doesn't necessarily mean that race relations in the United States have improved. Just because white people admire Michael Jordan doesn't mean that they will treat other African Americans with respect. And when minority athletes step out of their uniforms, they remember what it means to be a minority in America.

Should famous athletes like Michael Jordan do more to help the African-American community? Many people think so.

A LEVEL PLAYING FIELD

THE END OF APARTHEID

Black South African athletes are making a journey toward equality similar to that of African-American athletes. In South Africa, the Olympic hopes of black athletes can become a reality. But that wasn't always the case.

For decades, black athletes in South Africa could only dream of competing in the Olympics. The sports world had closed its doors to South Africa. The end of apartheid—a government policy that gave power to the minority white population in South Africa—was the only key to reopening those doors.

The case of South Africa shows how the sports community helped end an unjust policy. Sports organizations worldwide protested apartheid. One of the most significant challenges came when the International Olympic Committee banned South Africa from the 1964 Games.

The 1992 South African Olympic team

In 1968 the IOC reversed its position, in light of progress South Africa had made toward improving sports facilities for the majority black population.

But more than 40 countries threatened to boycott the 1968 Games, and several African-American athletes, including basketball player Kareem Abdul-Jabbar (then known as Lew Alcindor), boycotted the Olympic trials. Responding to international pressure, the IOC reversed its decision and didn't issue another invitation to South Africa until the 1992 Games.

By 1992 South African President F. W. de Klerk had recognized the African National Congress, the nation's leading black political party. The country was moving toward a new constitution that would grant political rights to people of all races. When the veil of apartheid lifted off South Africa, the sports world responded. After a 32-year absence from the Olympics, South Africa was allowed to send an integrated team to the 1992 Games. Though most of the 97-member team was white, black athletes finally could represent South Africa.

Many protested the IOC's decision to readmit South Africa, saying that the move had come too soon. South Africa had promised to create a program to help black, Indian, Asian, and mixed-race athletes become more competitive. But that program had barely gotten under way before the 1992 Games. "Simply allowing blacks to compete in sports isn't good enough when they go home and are treated like slaves," said Edwin Moses, a two-time Olympic gold medalist for the United States.[5]

Indeed, the struggle is not over for black athletes in South Africa. With little food to eat, squalid living conditions, and violence surrounding them, black athletes have little more than dreams to work with. Many have no equipment, training facilities, or coaches. But they refuse to give in to despair.

That black South Africans have been given a chance to compete alongside white South Africans says a lot about the country's movement to heal race relations. In April 1994, black South Africans voted for the first time in history. Nelson Mandela, head of the ANC, became the nation's first black president. Still, racial divisions in South Africa run deep. Achieving equality in sports and politics will take years of work.

For instance, fame provided no cushion for Boston Celtic guard Dee Brown. As he was sitting in his car, parked across the street from a bank, Boston police officers, with their guns drawn, forced him to get out of the car and lie on the pavement while they searched him. The police had received a call from a bank employee who suspected that Dee Brown was the black man who had robbed the bank earlier that week.

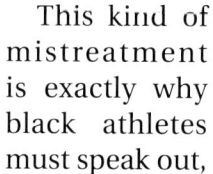

This kind of mistreatment is exactly why black athletes must speak out, many say. But others say that even if minority athletes don't take stands on issues, they are nevertheless doing their part for social change. Their ability to appeal to people of all races helps race relations, many argue.

Regardless of whether they choose to take a stand on issues, athletes are role models. They're admired for their talent, fame, and wealth, and they're idols for young people who see sports as a pathway to a better life. Role models of any kind are put up to impossibly high standards. They're expected to walk a tightrope of good behavior, and it's inevitable that some will fall off.

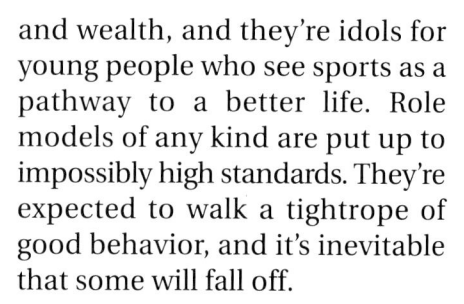

Some people agree with Charles Barkley and reject the role model job. Others embrace it. In a *Sports Illustrated* editorial, the Utah Jazz's Karl Malone explained, "I don't think we can accept all the glory and the money that comes with being a famous athlete and not accept the responsibility of being a role model, of knowing that kids and even some adults are watching us and looking for us to set an example. I mean, why do we get endorsements in the first place? Because there are people who will follow our lead and buy a certain sneaker or cereal because we use it."[6]

Athletes such as Jackie Robinson, Muhammad Ali, and Bill Russell weren't satisfied with making contributions only in athletics. They used their fame and stature to work for a greater good in society. Jim Brown has received almost as much acclaim for his work with inner-city gang members as he has for his accomplishments

Jackie Joyner-Kersee

on the football field. Heptathlon champion Jackie Joyner-Kersee established the Jackie Joyner-Kersee Foundation to help youths in poor inner-city neighborhoods.

Arthur Ashe also set the standard for political involvement. After becoming the first black man to win the Wimbledon tennis tournament, he signed endorsement deals with Head sports equipment company. But tennis made up just one aspect of Ashe's life. He campaigned and even went to jail for causes he believed in, protesting apartheid in South Africa and the U.S. immigration policy for Haitian refugees. He became a devoted advocate for racial equality in sports, examining the role of black athletes in history in several books. He never backed down, and he became a passionate voice for racial justice.

In September 1992, Arthur Ashe was arrested while protesting the treatment of Haitian refugees.

CHAPTER FIVE
BROKEN PROMISES

When Kevin Ross played basketball for Creighton University in Nebraska, he scored on the court but not in the classroom. After three years at Creighton, he could read at only the second-grade level. "Kevin couldn't even figure out what the average score of a game was. He just knew if they were ahead or behind," said Daniel Wolff, Ross's lawyer.[1]

He later enrolled in an elementary school to learn how to read. His teacher, Marva Collins, astonished that Ross had advanced to college without basic academic skills, found that secretaries had typed Ross's papers and that he had gotten through college taking courses such as first aid.

Cases like Kevin Ross's may be unusual, but the low graduation rates of athletes in Division I colleges are not. The reality behind college sports, specifically basketball and football, is a culture filled with exploitation, racism, neglect, and falsified records.

College athletics is big business. And universities have been accused of exploiting the hopes and talents of many black student-athletes, using them to draw big ticket sales, alumni donations, and network television contracts. But student-athletes are not always getting something in return. Many don't graduate and others leave college with little education and no hope for a professional career in sports or any other field.

BIG MONEY ON CAMPUS

Companies such as Nike and Reebok pay coaches millions of dollars to outfit their players with brand-name shoes and clothing. College athletic departments get rich from television contracts. With so much money at stake, it can be hard to let poor grades and NCAA rules stand in the way of winning. Coaches have been known to ignore student-athletes' drug problems or poor academic performances just to keep them on the team. The most serious charges of wrongdoing involve paying student-athletes and falsifying records to keep them from flunking out.

In his book *Personal Fouls,* Peter Golenbock charges that North Carolina State basketball players received illegal gifts of cars and

University football programs make vast sums of money—sometimes neglecting players' educations in the process.

money. Professors gave good grades to athletes who hadn't earned them.

NCAA officials say that black athletes are most often involved in these cases of wrongdoing. "Superior athletes with poor academic backgrounds are the ones we find in our serious cases," said the NCAA's David Berst. "An individual who only has a dream of the pros is more likely to fall victim" to corruption. [2]

Often dreams are all black student-athletes have. Many have meager educations and come from poor families. They're taught from an early age that sports is the ticket to success. Coaches and colleges feed this idea to young athletes, often beginning to recruit them in junior high.

When Billy Harris was a star athlete in high school in 1969, he lived a different life from other students. He was courted by colleges with free lunches, clothes, and money. By his junior year in high school, star basketball player Chris Washburn had received two large boxes full of letters from colleges. Recruiters promised to make him an All-American and a first-round NBA draft pick if he would attend their school.

But such promises are often far from reality. Only 1,000 out of every 10,000 high school athletes will play in college, and only 1 athlete out of that same 10,000 will become a professional. Arthur Ashe noted that too many high school students see sports as the road to success, despite the odds against them. They bank on an unrealistic dream of going pro when they have a much better chance of becoming a doctor or lawyer. Students aren't motivated to study or explore realistic career options, Ashe explained, when they're blinded by the glitter of professional sports.

"The exploitation of black athletes by colleges and universities in this country has been going on for a long time, even at a school with the history and reputation of USC," says Marvin Cobb, assistant athletic director at the University of Southern California. "USC, like many schools, is a virtual black-athlete factory running on quarter speed. They go out and sell those kids on the Trojan family, that a USC degree will mean the world. Yet they don't . . . make it an even chance for the kids they recruit."[3]

By the time student-athletes are in college, they're a little closer to realizing their dreams of going

SPORTS AND RACE

pro. But many of these students aren't being shown other job options besides those in athletics. About 75 percent of student-athletes major in physical education and related subjects.

MAKING THE GRADE

When Chris Washburn took the Scholastic Aptitude Test (SAT), he answered only a few questions and fell asleep during the test. He figured he didn't need a good score: Colleges and coaches had been courting him since he was 14. Later, Washburn's score of 470 on his SAT became public. Test-takers earn 400 points by merely signing their names on the test.

In 1986 the NCAA enacted a rule that would keep students like Washburn from entering college without the proper academic skills. Known as Proposition 48, the rule set up academic standards for athletes. It was intended to show student-athletes that studying is just as important as playing sports.

Under Proposition 48, students need a 2.0 grade-point average in several high school level courses and a score of 700 on the SAT or 15 on the American College Testing exam to play or practice on a college team. Those athletes who don't make the grade must sit out of sports until they do. The rule was followed up several years later with Proposition 42, which

As a freshman at Memphis State University, Anfernee Hardaway didn't meet Proposition 48 standards. He improved his grades and went on to a pro basketball career.

withheld scholarships from students who didn't meet Proposition 48's standards.

The NCAA rules have drawn criticism and praise. Many say that Proposition 48 is moving athletics in the right direction. It places education higher on a student-athlete's list of priorities, helping those who won't beat the odds of going pro.

Student-athletes should be getting an education—no one disputes that. But some people argue that Proposition 48 isn't the right solution. According to the American Institutes for Research, 90 percent of Proposition 48 students are black. Critics say that the rule discriminates against African Americans, especially those from disadvantaged backgrounds.

Black professors and leaders such as Jesse Jackson have protested the rule, charging that it punishes black student-athletes before they can prove themselves in the college classroom. They criticize Proposition 48 for using randomly set academic standards and for placing too much emphasis on the SAT. Scoring well on the test requires knowing a lot about white middle-class culture, critics say, and white test-takers have the advantage.

Critics also say that Proposition 48 doesn't address the real problems facing student-athletes. Once on campus, they become part of an athlete subculture, isolated from other students, and they receive little support in their academic classes. Critics of Proposition 48 say that tutoring programs for student-athletes are often low budget and offer minimal aid.

Students forced to sit out from athletics until they improve their grades also bear the burden of being "Prop 48." When Anfernee Hardaway graduated from high school in Memphis, Tennessee, he was arguably the best high school basketball player in the country. But he sat out during his first year at Memphis State University because of Proposition 48. "People think I'm dumb," he told *Sports Illustrated*. "I get it from both sides. Some people here—but brothers from the 'hood do it, too."[4]

Hardaway played with the Tigers the next season, the result of his near B-average work. He surpassed Proposition 48 standards, making the dean's list three times. But many student-athletes don't. Only 35 percent of black male athletes graduate from college in six years, according to a 1992 NCAA study. Black female athletes fare a little better, graduating at a rate of 43 percent.

A PASSIONATE DEBATE

Proposition 48 supporters say that student-athletes need special treatment, and that's precisely why the rule is necessary. It forces student-athletes to study. And sitting out a year gives athletes a chance to be regular students, free of athletic and team pressures. Proposition 48 "isn't such a bad idea," said Rumeal Robinson, who sat out his first year at the University of Michigan and later played in the NBA. "It works well for kids who didn't get that good an education in high school. It gives them a chance to meet people on campus, to see things that they probably wouldn't see if they were playing sports, to be a normal student."[5] Robinson became an All-American and graduated with degrees in communications and kinesiology.

One of Proposition 48's most ardent supporters is Harry Edwards, now a professor of sociology at the University of California at Berkeley. He is best known for his role in spurring the black protest at the 1968 Olympics. But he was also an athlete who could barely read or write when he left the inner city for the chance to play on a college team. He criticizes Proposition 48 for not being strict enough. If anything, its standards are so low that they insult student-athletes, Edwards says. He thinks higher standards would better prepare athletes for life after sports. Without academic skills, these athletes may not be better off after college than they were when they started.

Penn State football coach Joe Paterno joined Edwards in supporting Proposition 48. "For 15 years, we have had a race problem," he says. "We have raped a generation and a half of young

Harry Edwards

Georgetown coach John Thompson said that Proposition 42 specifically hurt black athletes.

black athletes. We have taken kids and sold them on bouncing a ball and running with a football and that being able to do certain things athletically was going to be an end in itself. We cannot afford to do that to another generation."⁶

The debate over Proposition 48 became explosive with the passage of Proposition 42, the rule that withdrew scholarship money from Proposition 48 athletes. Eighty-eight percent of black student-athletes are on scholarship.

By withholding money from those who didn't qualify, critics said, Proposition 42 made a college education increasingly unavailable to black student-athletes. Critics also charged that the measure encouraged student-athletes to accept illegal cash gifts as a way to stay in school.

One critic of Proposition 42 was Tony Rice, a quarterback who led Notre Dame to the national title in 1988. He showed that he had potential in school and on the field. He majored in psychology and later became a purchasing agent for an Illinois manufacturing company. Rice scored a 690 on the SAT, just below the standard set by Proposition 48. He believes that under Proposition 42, he and other low-income black student-athletes wouldn't have been able to attend college.

Georgetown basketball coach John Thompson passionately denounced Proposition 42, walking off the court in protest before a game with rival Boston College in January 1989. He said the rule was racist, designed to lock low-income blacks out of college sports. Thompson and others saw the measure as an effort by whites to keep the number of black student-athletes from becoming too high.

Proposition 42 was repealed at a 1990 NCAA convention. But the debate over Proposition 48 continues. Joe Paterno says that coaches have seen the academic caliber of high school athletes improve since the rule was passed. But academic performances haven't improved much for college athletes, and for every success story, there's a failure. For every student-athlete who sees athletics as a path to a college education, there's another banking on an ill-fated dream of going pro. And for every coach who makes sure his or her players are making the grade, there's another who will get an "academically risky" student-athlete into college at whatever cost.

STUDENTS OR CELEBRITIES?

Billy Thompson never thought he would have a career in professional football. So it came as a surprise when he was drafted by the Denver Broncos from mostly black Maryland State University. He went on to a career with the Broncos and now is director of alumni relations for the team.

While he was in school, he says, he "tried to experience the whole

A LEVEL PLAYING FIELD

college deal . . . I wanted to teach school, and I wanted to get my degree. Those were the things that were most important to me. Sports was important to me, but it wasn't the most important thing. If I hadn't been drafted, I don't think I would've been that disappointed." [7]

Thompson was very involved in campus life, but his experience is rare for many black student-athletes. Because athletics takes up so much time, student-athletes often feel isolated from student life. The experience can be especially lonely for black athletes at mostly white colleges, where they are isolated by their athletic role and also by their race.

Many student-athletes become famous before they ever leave college, as did several of these Duke University basketball players.

INTEGRATING THE SEC

In 1967, as the first black basketball player in the Southeastern Conference, Perry Wallace broke through a longstanding barrier in college sports. Integration wouldn't happen in this conference without a struggle. Wallace enrolled at Vanderbilt University in Nashville and played basketball under extraordinary circumstances. Racial abuse and vicious waving of Confederate flags were the norm.

"Only after I graduated and left Nashville did I realize how much was at stake emotionally and psychologically," he said. "There was so much at risk that...I could have been consumed by fear and pain, but I fought to overcome that." [8]

Wallace's breakthrough led to the gradual integration of the Southeastern Conference, which is now mostly black. Before the SEC integrated, most black athletes in the South went to all-black colleges. These were the only schools that would offer black athletes scholarships and a chance to be seen by professional recruiters. Grambling in Louisiana, Jackson State in Mississippi, and Tennessee State were among the black colleges with strong athletic programs. They helped establish a black tradition in football and baseball.

But their athletic programs were poorly funded. Teachers often doubled as coaches to save money. Stadiums held fewer than 10,000 people, and some schools were forced to rent playing fields. Though these schools had small budgets and poor facilities, they produced winning teams.

As the SEC opened up to African Americans, the athletic programs at many black colleges crumbled. Athletes found that black colleges couldn't offer them the resources or national stature that larger, Division I schools could.

In recent years, many black colleges have revitalized their athletic programs. Football games between these schools now draw good-sized crowds, and the caliber of the teams has attracted NFL scouts and top coaches. These programs have also attracted star black athletes, many of whom turn down opportunities to attend Division I schools in exchange for a more comfortable atmosphere on campus.

In the 1960s, black student-athletes who enrolled at mostly white schools faced difficulties on and off the field. Finding a place to live was a constant problem, as white landlords often refused to rent to African Americans. Finding housing during road trips was also difficult. For a game in Houston, Oscar Robertson, the only black player on the University of Cincinnati basketball team, had to stay at a nearby black college. Those few black women who made college cheerleading squads were often kept from view, especially on television, for fear of angering wealthy team supporters.

During the social revolution in the 1960s, college campuses became hotbeds for change. And black student-athletes were more vocal in their demands for equality. Black students pushed for more black cheerleaders and equal treatment for black athletes. Their efforts brought tension, but in some cases, they brought results. When University of California basketball player Bob Presley was dropped from the team for refusing to cut his Afro-style hair, the university took action against the coach, eventually firing him.

The situation for black student-athletes in the 1990s has changed for the better, but feelings of isolation remain. In contrast with the past, privilege, not mistreatment, helps create this atmosphere of isolation. Highly visible because of their race, media exposure, and often their size, many black athletes are local celebrities. Some say they experience very little racism. Loy Vaught, who played on the University of Michigan basketball team, told the *New York Times*, "The only thing I see from any student is that they show admiration and they go out of their way to speak to me and make sure I feel comfortable when I'm around them." But, Vaught added, "I feel like I'm not really a part of what's going on with blacks on campus."[9]

Vaught was not alone. Many black athletes feel alienated from their school's black student body. In recent years, as racial issues have been raised on campuses, black student leaders have urged black student-athletes to speak out and use their popularity to help change campus policies. Athletes have been encouraged, for example, to help demonstrate for more funding for black organizations on campus.

But many athletes, contemplating a career in professional sports,

Black student-athletes say it's tough to attend mostly white schools.

fear that speaking out may hurt their future. They worry about losing their scholarships or being dropped from the team. Alex Strong, who played football for Auburn University, said, "I couldn't really change things, and even if I did try to start influencing these guys [the administration], they could just eliminate me."[10] On campus as in the pros, taking a stand on racial issues can ruin a career. Many student-athletes aren't willing to run the risk.

76 A LEVEL PLAYING FIELD

For decades, golf was off-limits to African Americans. Many barriers remain for minorities in the sport.

CHAPTER SIX

THE PRICE OF ADMISSION

On June 21, 1990, when Louis J. Willie stepped on the greens at Shoal Creek country club in Birmingham, Alabama, he made a small step forward for civil rights. Willie's gesture was quiet, but it pushed golf a large step forward toward racial equality. It called to mind the movement Rosa Parks set in motion when she refused to give up her seat on a bus to a white man in the same state in 1955.

Shoal Creek won't be remembered for its lush greens or its Jack Nicklaus-designed golf course. It will be remembered for its first black golfer, Louis Willie, and its owner, Hall Thompson. Shoal Creek was launched into notoriety when Thompson told a reporter from the Birmingham *Post-Herald* about the club's policy of not giving black people memberships: "Bringing up this issue will just polarize the community . . . but it can't pressure us. . . We have the right to associate or not to associate with whomever we choose. The country club is our home and we pick and choose who we want . . . I think we've said that we don't discriminate in every other area except the blacks."[1]

BATTLE LINES

The controversy over black membership at Shoal Creek was not the first in golf. In the early part of the century, most golf courses were segregated. As the number of black golfers rose after World War II, black courses became overcrowded. Many black golfers tried to join clubs that were exclusively white.

Denied access to these clubs, black golfers took their battles to court. In 1948 three prominent black golfers challenged a PGA ruling that said only white golfers could join the association. Bill Spiller, Ted Rhodes, and Madison Gunter sued the PGA and the Richmond (California) Golf Club for denying them membership. The PGA said it would drop its exclusionary policy if the lawsuit were dropped. The suit was dropped, but the PGA continued to exclude black golfers. The association changed the name of its tournaments from "opens" to "invitationals"—and then invited only white golfers to enter.

More lawsuits followed. One reached the Supreme Court: Golfer Jim Rice sued a Florida country club that allowed black golfers on its public course only one day a week. The Florida Supreme Court upheld the club's right to restrict black golfers, and the case went before the federal Supreme Court in March 1950. Eight months later, the high court overturned the Florida court ruling. That victory set off a tide of legal action across the country. Some cities created more courses for black golfers. Others desegregated public courses.

The legal effort not only hastened integration in sports, but also pushed integration in general. The National Association for the Advancement of Colored People sponsored the drive against golf course segregation, realizing that a court ruling in its favor would help black people gain access to more public facilities.

SPORTS AND RACE

Thompson's remarks aroused the anger of the black community. He apologized for his comments, and many prominent golfers came to his defense. Still, civil rights groups demanded that the Professional Golfer's Association cancel a tournament at the club to protest its racist practices. The golf industry responded to Thompson's comments with self-examination. The remarks brought attention to discrimination throughout the sport.

Changes came within weeks after Thompson's remarks. A sense of fairness wasn't what sparked the change. Instead, money helped set the stage for the transformation. Corporate America hurried to create some distance from the controversy. Wealthy sponsors such as Anheuser-Busch, Lincoln-Mercury, and IBM refused to buy advertising time on ABC's broadcast of the Shoal Creek tournament. Toyota recommended that its spokespeople, including Lee Trevino, not wear the Toyota logo at the tournament. Shortly afterward, the PGA said that it would not hold tournaments at clubs that had discriminatory membership policies. The Ladies Professional Golf Association created a similar policy.

Some clubs withdrew from the PGA tour. Others that had had all-white memberships announced that they were willing to accept black members. And as a result of the incident, golf pro Jim Thorpe founded the Minority Golf Foundation, aimed at introducing inner-city youths to golf. Country clubs can remain on the PGA tour if they have just one black member. But the tour maintains that its

Lee Trevino

A LEVEL PLAYING FIELD

The 1992 U.S. Olympic swim team. Why do so few minority youths excel in competitive swimming?

SPORTS AND RACE

goal is to have a significant minority presence in golf, not just token members.

HIGH-END ATHLETICS

Clubs like Shoal Creek never had much incentive to change their discriminatory policies, because there simply aren't many minority golfers. Only two percent of the black population plays golf. This fact points to a larger question that has plagued sports for years: Why are there so many minorities in track and field, basketball, football, and baseball but so few in sports such as gymnastics, figure skating, hockey, skiing, swimming, golf, and tennis?

Many minority youths aren't interested in skiing and tennis because minority role models in these sports are rare. Few have the popularity of a Magic Johnson or Michael Jordan. But the main reason that minority youths don't play certain sports is economic. Playing tennis, for example, requires a lot of money. Rackets are expensive. So is traveling to tournaments, which often take place at white suburban tennis clubs and can be uncomfortable events for minority athletes from inner cities.

BALL FIELDS GONE BY

Black children once revered baseball heroes like Jackie Robinson and Hank Aaron and longed to excel in the big leagues. In recent years, black participation in baseball has declined, in part because of the rising popularity of basketball. Fewer black players are entering baseball and the game is losing black fans. Black youths, seeing fewer black athletes on the field in key positions, say that baseball is a "white man's sport."

A Boston University study showed that baseball teams that moved their stadiums from 1950 to 1970 moved from mostly black neighborhoods to ones that had fewer black residents. In Atlanta, where the population is 60 percent black, only about 4 percent of baseball tickets are sold to black fans. St. Louis has a similar problem, selling just 3 percent of tickets to African Americans.

As baseball and black communities have moved further apart, some teams have made an effort to bring the sport back to these communities. From youth programs that rebuild ball fields in inner cities to increased advertising on black-oriented media, baseball is trying to shake its reputation of racial exclusion. Recently, major-league baseball decided to give health insurance to surviving players of the Negro leagues, who never saw many rewards for what they gave to the game.

Baseball fans—mostly a white crowd

A costly sport, skiing is dominated by white athletes.

Arthur Ashe, who worked to bring tennis to urban youths, said the problem goes much deeper: "Blacks have basically been tolerated in tennis. As long as there aren't too many of us, it's okay. The American tennis community, and white society in general, is afraid that if we get our foot in the door, we'll do in tennis what we've done in basketball—take over. It's the same with other individual sports like gymnastics or swimming. They're all preserves of the white upper middle class."[2]

The situation in golf is similar. Ever since Charlie Sifford became the first black golfer to play in PGA tournaments in 1961, the number of minority golfers hasn't gone much beyond a token few. Before Sifford, golf was largely off-limits to minorities, because many clubs and the PGA had policies of admitting only whites.

Today, the barriers are still there, but they're less apparent. Inner-city athletic programs, strapped for cash, rarely offer golf. Though a lot of clubs have lifted their

African-American teenagers go all out at a high school track contest.

exclusionary membership policies, minorities still are locked out. Most golf courses are located in white suburban areas, far away from the inner cities. Playing a round of golf or learning the game requires an expensive set of clubs and costly lessons. Country club memberships cost tens of thousands of dollars.

"Not enough minority kids are learning golf at an early age. So when they get to college, they're not competitive," says Tina White, executive director of the Calvin Peete Golf Foundation, which brings golf to inner-city youths. "Many kids from the city are never exposed to things outside their own neighborhood."[3]

SPORTS AND RACE

TRENDS IN BASEBALL

Hispanics were playing professional baseball long before Jackie Robinson integrated the game. Light-skinned Cubans played in the major leagues, but Hispanic athletes with darker skin weren't allowed in the leagues before Robinson. Today Hispanic athletes have become such a force in baseball that all major-league teams now have scouts in Puerto Rico and recruit players from Colombia, Nicaragua, Venezuela, Panama, and Mexico.

Toronto's Roberto Alomar—a native of Puerto Rico

In contrast, black athletes have become dominant in track, basketball, football, and baseball because these sports are accessible to people of all income levels. Urban playgrounds and school yards have produced some of the world's greatest ballplayers. In the post–World War II period, basketball has thrived in black communities. The sport calls for minimal equipment: a basketball, shoes, and a court. Most African-American youths have a basketball court within walking distance. And there isn't much coaching required: Once players learn basic offensive moves, they can play the game.

WHO CAN COMPETE?

Sports can be a ticket out of poverty for a lucky few. But poverty keeps many other minority athletes from reaching their potential in sports. Golfer Lee Trevino, who broke into the sport in the 1960s, says that modern Hispanic

Basketball is increasingly popular in African-American communities.

students have a lot of pressure on them to drop out, use drugs, and join gangs. "If I was growing up with today's peer pressure, I don't think I would've made it," he says.[4]

The lack of Native Americans in sports also may be due to a high dropout rate. "We don't have the opportunities that non-Indian people have for scholarships," said Clyde Bellecourt. "We have a high dropout rate in high schools because schools don't stress Indian culture and tradition . . . and we don't have the money to go to colleges and compete."[5]

Dropout rates for black students are often just as high, and many black athletes struggle with the same obstacles presented by drugs and street gangs. But recruiters, keen on discovering the next Shaquille O'Neal or Emmitt Smith, keep an eye on inner-city gymnasiums and ballparks and often usher promising student-athletes through to graduation. The desire to be a big-ticket player keeps some minority athletes in school. Although the dream of going pro may be a false promise for most, sports might still lead them to a college education and career opportunities off the playing field.

The struggle for equality in sports is not over. But the progress that has been made in this century is undeniable. The history of minorities in 20th-century sports is a tale of the triumph of the human spirit. Countless athletes and pioneers made history through the record books; others did so through integrity, suffering, perseverance, compassion, and sheer will. Through their efforts and accomplishments, each of these individuals laid the foundation for a brighter future for the athletes who follow them.

NOTES

CHAPTER 1: BREAKING THE COLOR BARRIER
1. Shelley Smith, "Remembering Their Game," *Sports Illustrated*, 6 July, 1992, 91.
2. Kenny Moore, "A Courageous Stand," *Sports Illustrated*, 5 August 1991, 66.
3. Ibid., 68.
4. Milton Jamail, "Major League Bucks," *Hispanic*, April 1993, 18–22.

CHAPTER 2: TYPECASTING
1. Richard Lapchick, "Pseudo-Scientific Prattle about Athletes," *New York Times*, 29 April 1989.
2. Martin Kane, "An Assessment of 'Black is Best,'" *Sports Illustrated*, 18 January 1971, 72–83.
3. Lapchick, "Pseudo-Scientific Prattle."
4. Mark Maske, "O's Scout Apologizes," *Washington Post*, 26 February 1993, F4.
5. Derrick Z. Jackson, "Sports Broadcasting; Calling the Plays in Black and White," *Boston Globe*, 22 January 1989, A25.
6. Rick Reilly, "Let's Bust Those Chops," *Sports Illustrated*, 28 October 1991, 110.
7. Clyde Bellecourt, interview with author, 18 September 1993.
8. Brad Knickerbocker, "Rooting Out Remnants of Racism," *The Christian Science Monitor*, 18 March 1992.

CHAPTER 3: WHO'S IN CHARGE?
1. William Oscar Johnson, "A Matter of Black and White," *Sports Illustrated*, 5 August 1991, 46.
2. Jack Olsen, "In the Back of the Bus," *Sports Illustrated*, July 22, 1968, 39.
3. Ibid., 39.
4. Mark Maske, "Baseball Suspends Schott 1 Year for Racial Slurs." *Washington Post*, 4 February 1993, A1, A4.
5. Claire Smith, Gerald Eskenazi, and William Rhoden, "Too Few Changes Since Campanis," *New York Times*, 16 August 1992, sec. 8, p.1.
6. Ibid.
7. Lynn Rosellini et al., "Strike One and You're Out," *U.S. News & World Report*, 27 July 1987, 52.
8. Jeffrey Benedict, interview with author, 24 September 1993.
9. William Reed, "Equality Begins at Home," *Sports Illustrated*, 26 November 1990, 138.
10. Ken Denlinger, "America's Sports Still Lag in Race," *Washington Post*, 7 February 1993, D1.

11. Smith, Eskenazi, and Rhoden, "Too Few Changes."

12. Norman Chad, "Balance of Power Affects Balance of Color," *Washington Post*, 22 June 1989, B1, B11.

CHAPTER 4: BEYOND THE PLAYING FIELD

1. Joanne Lipman, "Is Commercial Field Level for Black Athletes?" *Wall Street Journal*, reprinted in *St. Petersburg Times*, 25 October 1988, 1D.

2. Laura Zinn, "To Marketers, Kristi Yamaguchi Isn't as Good as Gold," *Business Week*, 9 March 1992, 40.

3. Associated Press, "Jordan Backs Some of Hodges' Criticism of Athletes' Priorities," *Saint Paul Pioneer Press*, 5 June 1992.

4. E. M. Swift, "Reach Out and Touch Someone," *Sports Illustrated*, 5 August 1991, 58.

5. Roy Johnson, "Don't Let up on Pretoria," *Sports Illustrated*, 26 February 1990, 92.

6. Karl, Malone, "One Role Model to Another," *Sports Illustrated*, 14 June 1993, 84.

CHAPTER 5: BROKEN PROMISES

1. Jack Kroll et al., "Race Becomes the Game," *Newsweek*, 30 January 1989, 56–59.

2. Ibid.

3. Phil Taylor and Shelley Smith. "Exploitation or Opportunity," *Sports Illustrated*, 12 August 1991, 47.

4. Ralph Wiley, "A Daunting Proposition," *Sports Illustrated*, 12 August 1991, 28.

5. Ibid., 33.

6. Harry Edwards, "Educating Black Athletes," *Atlantic Monthly*, August, 1983, 33.

7. Billy Thompson, interview with author, October 1993.

8. William F. Reed, "Culture Shock in Dixieland," *Sports Illustrated*, August 12, 1991, 54.

9. William C. Rhoden, "Black Student-Athletes Find Life of Privilege and Isolation," *New York Times*, 8 January 1990, A1, C4.

10. Ibid.

CHAPTER 6: THE PRICE OF ADMISSION

1. William Oscar Johnson, "The Gates Open," *Sports Illustrated*, 13 August 1990, 54–57.

2. Roger Williams, "Is Tennis Doing the Right Thing for Blacks?" *Tennis*, November 1990, 46–50.

3. Leonard Shapiro and Tony Reid, "Shoal Creek: A Wave, Then a Trickle," *Washington Post*, 6 August 1991, D1, D3.

4. Martha Frase-Blunt, "Getting into the Game," *Hispanic*, January/February 1993, 32.

5. Clyde Bellecourt, interview with author, 18 September 1993.

SELECTED BIBLIOGRAPHY

Adler, Jerry. "Good Field, No Pitch." *Newsweek,* April 12, 1993.

Ashe, Arthur. "Can Blacks Beat the Old-Boy Network?" *Newsweek,* January 27, 1992.

——————. *Hard Road to Glory.* New York: Warner Books Inc., 1988.

Bellecourt, Clyde. Interview with author. September 18, 1993.

Benedict, Jeffrey. Interview with author. September 24, 1993.

Chambers, Marcia. "The Fallout from Shoal Creek." *Golf Digest,* January 1991.

Crothers, Tim. "Can Black Golfers Come to the Fore?" *Sports Illustrated,* July 9, 1990.

DeFrantz, Anita. "We've Got to Be Strong." *Sports Illustrated,* August 12, 1991.

Edwards, Harry. "Educating Black Athletes." *The Atlantic Monthly,* August 1983.

Evans, David. "The Wrong Examples." *Newsweek,* March 1, 1993.

Farrell, Charles. "Black Collegiate Athletes Are Being Doublecrossed." *USA Today* magazine, November 1990.

——————. "Minority Concerns, Gender Equity Pondered as Part of NCAA Certification." *Black Issues in Higher Education,* July 2, 1992.

——————. "NCAA Study Shows Black Male Athletes Far Behind in Graduation Rates." *Black Issues in Higher Education,* July 30, 1992.

Gates, Henry Louis Jr. "Delusions of Grandeur." *Sports Illustrated,* August 19, 1991.

Giago, Tim. "I Hope the Redskins Lose." *Newsweek,* January 27, 1992.

Hammer, Joshua, Manly, Howard, and Mabry, Marcus. "Business as Usual." *Newsweek,* January 27, 1992.

Henderson, Edwin B. and the editors of *Sport* magazine. *The Black Athlete: Emergence and Arrival.* Cornwells Heights, Pennsylvania: The Publishers Agency Inc., 1976.

Hickok, Ralph. *The Encyclopedia of North American Sports History.* New York: Facts on File Inc., 1992.

Hirschfelder, Arlene. *American Indian Stereotypes in the World of Children: a Reader and Bibliography.* Metuchen, New Jersey: Scarecrow Press Inc., 1982.

Hoffer, Richard. "Too Hot to Handle." *Sports Illustrated,* May 11, 1992.

Holway, John. *Voices from the Great Black Baseball Leagues.* New York: Da Capo Press, 1992.

Jamail, Milton. "Major League Bucks." *Hispanic,* April 1993.

Johnson, Joseph and Ashe, Arthur. "Is Proposition 48 Racist?" *Ebony,* June 1989.

Johnson, Roy. "Don't Let up on Pretoria." *Sports Illustrated,* February 26, 1990.

Johnson, William Oscar. "The Gates Open." *Sports Illustrated,* August 13, 1990.

——————. "How Far Have We Come?" *Sports Illustrated,* August 5, 1991.

——————. "A Matter of Black and White." *Sports Illustrated,* August 5, 1991.

——————. "Welcome Back." *Sports Illustrated,* August 3, 1992.

Kane, Martin. "An Assessment of 'Black Is Best.'" *Sports Illustrated,* January 18, 1971.

Katz, Donald, "Triumph of the Swoosh." *Sports Illustrated,* August 16, 1993.

Kroll, Jack et al. "Race Becomes the Game." *Newsweek,* January 30, 1989.

Ladson, William. "Hank Aaron." *Sport,* February 1993.

Lapchick, Richard. *Five Minutes to Midnight: Race and Sport in the 1990s.* Lanham, Maryland: Madison Books, 1991.

Lapchick, Richard et al. "1992 Racial Report Card." Boston: Center for the Study of Sport in Society, Northeastern University. Photocopy.

Lapchick, Richard and Benedict, Jeffrey. "1994 Racial Report Card." Boston: Center for the Study of Sport in Society, Northeastern University. Photocopy.

Levin, Gary. "Baseball's Endorsement Shutout." *Advertising Age,* February 15, 1993.

Liesse, Julie and Jensen, Jeff. "Whole New Game without Jordan." *Advertising Age,* October 11, 1993.

Malone, Karl. "One Role Model to Another." *Sports Illustrated,* June 14, 1993.

McRae, F. Finley. "Hidden Traps Beneath Placid Greens." *American Visions,* April 1991.

Montville, Leigh. "Beantown: One Tough Place to Play." *Sports Illustrated,* August 19, 1991.

Moore, Kenny. "A Courageous Stand." *Sports Illustrated,* August 5, 1991.

——————. "The Eye of the Storm." *Sports Illustrated,* August 12, 1991.

Orr, Jack. *The Black Athlete: His Story in American History.* Scarsdale, New York: Lion Books, 1969.

Pewewardy, Cornel. "Native American Mascots and Imagery: the Struggle of Unlearning Indian Stereotypes." *Journal of Navajo Education,* Fall 1991.

Purkey, Mike. "Shoal Creek." *Golf Magazine,* August 1991.

Rainville, Raymond and McCormick, Edward. "Extent of Covert Racial Prejudice in Pro Football Announcers' Speech." *Journalism Quarterly,* Spring 1977.

Reed, William. "Culture Shock in Dixieland." *Sports Illustrated,* August 12, 1991.

———. "Equality Begins at Home." *Sports Illustrated,* November 26, 1990.

Reilly, Rick. "Let's Bust Those Chops." *Sports Illustrated,* October 28, 1991.

Rosellini, Lynn et al. "Strike One and You're Out." *U.S. News & World Report,* July 27, 1987.

Schapp, Richard. *An Illustrated History of the Olympics.* New York: Alfred A. Knopf, Inc., 1993.

Smith, Gary. "As Time Runs Out." *Sports Illustrated,* January 11, 1993.

Smith, Shelley. "Baseball's Forgotten Pioneers." *Sports Illustrated,* March 30, 1992.

———. "Remembering Their Game." *Sports Illustrated,* July 6, 1992.

Starr, Mark, Barrett, Todd, and Smith, Vern. "Baseball's Black Problem." *Newsweek,* July 19, 1993.

Swift, E. M. "Reach Out and Touch Someone." *Sports Illustrated,* August 5, 1991.

Taylor, Phil and Smith, Shelley. "Exploitation or Opportunity?" *Sports Illustrated,* August 12, 1991.

Telander, Rick. "Hard Time, Hard Questions." *Sports Illustrated,* December 24, 1990.

———. "Life Lessons from a Man of Steel." *Sports Illustrated,* August 19, 1991.

Thompson, Billy. Interview with author. October 1993.

Waldman, Steven and Bingham, Clara. "Sports, Race and Politics." *Newsweek,* August 17, 1992.

Weinstock, Jeff. "Blacked Out." *Sport,* March 1992.

Wiley, Ralph. "A Daunting Proposition." *Sports Illustrated,* August 12, 1991.

Williams, Roger. "Is Tennis Doing the Right Thing for Blacks?" *Tennis,* November 1990.

Zinn, Laura. "To Marketers, Kristi Yamaguchi Isn't as Good as Gold." *Business Week,* March 9, 1992.

INDEX

Aaron, Henry, 13, 25, 43, 59
Abdul-Jabbar, Kareem, 61
Ali, Muhammad, 20–21, 62
American College Testing exam, 67
American Indian Movement, 35
American Indians in sports. *See* Native Americans
Anson, Adrian "Cap," 14
Ashe, Arthur, 49, 63, 66, 83

Barkley, Charles, 37, 53, 56
baseball and minority participation, 24, 39, 82, 85. *See also* integration of baseball teams
basketball and minority participation, 24, 39, 86. *See also* integration of basketball teams
Beamon, Bob, 23
Bellecourt, Clyde, 35, 87
Benedict, Jeffrey, 44
Berst, David, 66
Black Coaches Association, 45–46
black colleges, 73
Bonilla, Bobby, 27
broadcasting. *See* media
Brooklyn Dodgers, 11, 12
Brown, Dee, 62
Brown, James, 46
Brown, Jim, 18, 54, 62
Brundage, Avery, 23

Calvin Peete Golf Foundation, 84
Campanis, Al, 29, 40
Carlos, John, 22–23, 57
Chamberlain, Wilt, 24
Chandler, Albert "Happy," 11
civil rights movement, 8, 11, 20, 74
Clay, Cassius. *See* Ali, Muhammad
Clifton, Nathaniel, 16
coaching and management positions, 40–46
Cobb, Marvin, 66
college sports programs: academic standards of, 64, 66–71; black athletes in, 66–75; coaching positions in, 45–46; integration of, 73, 74
Connors, Jimmy, 54
Cooper, Chuck, 16
Cuban Giants, 14
Cunningham, Randall, 27

de Klerk, F. W., 61
Doby, Larry, 39–40

Eastern Colored League, 14
economic barriers in sports, 81, 83, 84, 86–87
Edmundson, Ken, 46
Edwards, Harry, 23, 24, 50, 69
endorsements, 48–54

Falks, Frank, 45
football and minority participation, 30, 39, 86. *See also* integration of football teams
Foster, Andrew, 14
Fowler, Bud, 14

Gibson, Althea, 19
Golenbock, Peter, 65
golf and minority participation, 77, 78, 83–84
Grace, Willie, 14
Gunter, Madison, 78

Hardaway, Anfernee, 68
Harlem Globetrotters, 8, 17
Harris, Billy, 66
Head, Roger, 33
Hilliard, William, 35
Hines, Jim, 23
Hispanic athletes, 9, 31, 39, 85, 86
Hitler, Adolf, 6
Hodges, Craig, 58

integration: of baseball teams, 11–13, 15, 16; of basketball teams, 16; of college teams, 73, 74; of football teams, 18; of golf programs, 77, 78, 79

Jackson, Jessie, 46, 68
Johnson, Earvin "Magic," 48, 54
Johnson, Jack, 9
Jordan, Michael, 48, 50–51, 55, 58
Joyner-Kersee, Jackie, 63

Kerrigan, Nancy, 53
King, Martin Luther, Jr., 23

Ladies Professional Golf Assocation, 79
Lloyd, Earl, 16
Los Angeles riots, 54–55
Louis, Joe, 9–10, 49

McMahon, Jim, 50
McNamara, John, 43
Malone, Karl, 62
Mandela, Nelson, 61
media: jobs in, 46–47; treatment of athletes by, 28, 29, 30
Minneapolis *Star Tribune,* 35
Minority Golf Foundation, 79
Montreal Royals, 11–12
Moon, Warren, 27
Moses, Edwin, 61
Motley, Marion, 18

Native Americans: and sports participation, 9, 87; stereotypes of, 31–35
Negro leagues, 8, 11, 14–15, 82
Negro National League, 14
Nike shoe company, 50
Norman, Peter, 22
North Carolina State basketball team, 65–66

Olympic Games: and South Africa, 60–61; in Berlin (1936), 6; in Mexico City (1968), 22–23, 57
Olympic Project for Human Rights, 22
O'Neal, Shaquille, 53, 55
Owens, Jesse, 6, 8, 9, 23, 49

Paterno, Joe, 69–70, 71
Personal Fouls, 65–66
Polynice, Olden, 54
Portland *Oregonian,* 35
Presley, Bob, 74
Professional Golfer's Association, 78, 79, 83
Proposition 48, 67–71
Proposition 42, 67–68, 70–71

Racial Report Card, 30–31, 39, 46
Rainbow Commission for Fairness in Athletics, 46
reserve clause, 26, 27
Rhodes, Ted, 78
Rice, Jim, 78
Rice, Tony, 71
Richard, J. R., 30
Rickey, Branch, 12, 13
Robertson, Oscar, 74
Robinson, Frank, 40–41
Robinson, Jackie, 11–13, 15, 23, 62
Robinson, Rumeal, 69
Rodriguez, Rich, 39
Rose, Pete, 43
Ross, Kevin, 64
Rudolph, Wilma, 49
Russell, Bill, 24, 29, 62

salaries of minority athletes, 16, 26, 27
Scholastic Aptitude Test (SAT), 67, 68
Schott, Marge, 40
Shoal Creek golf club, 77
Shula, Dave, 44
Sifford, Charlie, 83
Simms, Phil, 50
Smith, Tommie, 22–23, 56–57
Snyder, Jimmy "the Greek," 40
South Africa and Olympic Games, 60–61
Southeastern Conference, 73
Spiller, Bill, 78
stacking, 24, 30–31
Stephen, Ted, 37–38
stereotypes: of minority athletes, 28–30; of Native Americans, 31–35
Strode, Woody, 18
Strong, Alex, 75

tennis and minority athletes, 19, 49, 81, 83
Thomas, Isiah, 58
Thompson, Billy, 71–72
Thompson, Hall, 77, 79

Thompson, John, 71
Thorpe, Jim (golf pro), 79
Thorpe, Jim (Native American athlete), 9
Torres, Jaime, 27
Trevino, Lee, 49–50, 79, 86–87
Tyus, Wyomia, 23

Uhlman, Fred, Sr., 29
University of Southern California, 66

Vaught, Loy, 74
Vietnam War, 20
Vincent, Fay, 46

Wallace, Perry, 73
Washburn, Chris, 66, 67
Washington, Kenny, 18
White, Tina, 84
Williams, Doug, 27, 50
Williams, Reggie, 43
Willie, Louis J., 77
Willis, Bill, 18
Wilson, Earl, 40
World War II, 10–11, 15

Yamaguchi, Kristi, 53

96 | **A LEVEL PLAYING FIELD**

ACKNOWLEDGMENTS

Photographs used with permission of UPI/Bettmann: pp. 2, 19, 21, 22, 57; Library of Congress: p. 7; National Baseball Library and Archive, Cooperstown, New York: pp. 9, 14, 15, 25; Pro Football Hall of Fame: pp. 10, 18; The Ring Book Shop, Madison Square Garden: p. 11; Brooklyn Dodgers: p. 12; D'Ambra Collection, University of Kansas, Lawrence: p. 16; Harlem Globetrotters International, Inc.: p. 17; *The Ring* magazine: p. 20; SportsChrome East/West, Robert Tringali Jr.: pp. 26, (left) 31, 36, 41, 65, 76, 79, 96; © Marc S. Levine, New York Mets: p. 26 (right); Durham Herald Co. Inc.: p. 29; SportsChrome East/West, Louis A. Raynor: p. 32; John Doman, St. Paul Pioneer Press: pp. 33, 34; © Mickey Pfleger: pp. 38, 45, 56, 59, 70, 85; Steve Lipofsky: pp. 39, 43; SportsChrome East/West, Rick Kane: p. 44; Lisa Hall, University of Oklahoma: p. 47; © Carol Newsom: p. 49; The Gatorade Company: p. 51; © Paul Harvath: p. 52; Pepsico Inc.: p. 55; Reuters/Bettmann: pp. 60, 63; SportsChrome East/West, Eileen Langsley: p. 62; Memphis State University: p. 67; Harry Edwards: p. 69; Duke Sports Information: p. 72; Wendell Vandersluis, University of Minnesota: p. 75; © Tim Morse: pp. 80, 81; SportsChrome East/West, Mike Kullen: p. 82; Hart Ski Company: p. 83; Lucille Sukalo: p. 84; SportsChrome East/West, Ron Wyatt: p. 86; SportsChrome East/West, Tim O'Lett: p. 93

Cover photograph: SportsChrome East/West, Jeff Carlick.